THE ULTIMATE BOOK OF
BONES

Written by **Jinny Johnson**

Illustrated by **Elizabeth Gray**
and **Steve Kirk**

BARNES
&NOBLE
B O O K S
NEW YORK

This edition published by Barnes & Noble Inc.,
by arrangement with Marshall Editions Ltd.

A Marshall Edition
Conceived, edited, and designed by
Marshall Editions Ltd
170 Piccadilly
London W1V 9DD

1998 Barnes and Noble Books

ISBN: 0 7607 0922 X

The Publishers would like to thank the Natural History
Museum, London, the Cambridge University Department
of Zoology, and the Royal Tyrrell Museum of
Palaeontology, Drumheller, Canada. The artist Elizabeth
Gray would like to thank Sandra Chapman at the British
Museum and Don Brinkman at the Royal Tyrrell
Museum for their help in the making of this book.

Editorial Director: Cynthia O'Brien
Managing Editor: Kate Phelps
Prehistoric Consultant: Dr. Barry Cox
Animal Consultant: Dr. Philip Whitfield
Design Manager: Ralph Pitchford
Research: Liz Ferguson, Jazz Wilson,
                             Simon Beecroft, Louise Owen
Production: Barry Baker, Janice Storr,
                             James Bann

Printed and bound in Italy

CONTENTS

INTRODUCTION

Pinch your arm or hand and you will feel the hard bones beneath your skin. Lots of different bones make up your skeleton, which is the support and framework for the body. Without bones, your body would be completely floppy. The bones also protect delicate parts of the body and make levers for movement.

Other animals, from fish and frogs to gorillas and great whales, have skeletons too. In the first section of this inside-outside look at animals, the skeletons of a range of creatures are examined in intricate detail. All the drawings have been made from real skeletons and they show how the bones in these amazing structures connect together.

Looking at skeletons also helps us to find out about animals of the past. Dinosaurs disappeared from the earth 60 million years ago. No human has ever seen a living dinosaur, but fossilized bones of many different kinds have been discovered. The second part of this book looks at the skeletons of dinosaurs and other prehistoric creatures. It includes an eight-page fold out of some of the largest dinosaurs—the biggest creatures ever to walk the earth.

The names of the prehistoric creatures are made up of Latin or Greek words that describe something about their appearance or behavior. The word dinosaur comes from the Greek for "terrible lizard." Here's how to say the names of the prehistoric animals in this book:

Ornitholestes:	*Orn-ith-oh-LEST-eez*
Gallimimus:	*Gal-lee-MEEM-us*
Dromaeosaurus:	*Dro-may-oh-SORE-us*
Tyrannosaurus:	*Tie-RAN-oh-sore-us*
Camarasaurus:	*Kam-ahra-SORE-us*

Diplodocus:	*Di-ploh-DOK-us*
Iguanodon:	*Ig-WHA-noh-don*
Lambeosaurus:	*LAM-bee-oh-sore-us*
Stegoceras:	*Steg-o-SER-as*
Stegosaurus:	*STEG-oh-sore-us*
Euoplocephalus:	*Yoo-op-loh-KEFF-ah-lus*
Triceratops:	*Try-SER-ah-tops*
Ichthyosaurs:	*IK-thee-oh-sores*
Plesiosaurs:	*PLEE-zee-oh-sores*
Pterosaurs:	*TER-oh-sores*
Archaeopteryx:	*Ar-kee-OP-ter-ix*

ATLANTIC COD

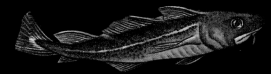

Fish were the first vertebrates—that means animals with backbones. The earliest fish lived about 500 million years ago. Since then four other groups of vertebrate animals—amphibians, reptiles, birds, and mammals—have developed. All have a backbone (also known as a spine) made up of individual bones called vertebrae. Backbones can be different lengths. Look at how many vertebrae a fish has compared to the short backbone of the frog on page 6.

All fish live in water. Some live in saltwater in the sea, others live in freshwater in rivers and lakes.

Each fin has many small bones called fin rays. These bones keep the fins stiff and spread out. The bones below the fins are called radials. They support the fins.

Bones over gills

Pectoral fins

Pelvic fins

Like all vertebrates, fish have a bony skull and a movable lower jaw. Special bones cover the gills on each side of a fish's head. Gills help a fish breathe in water. When we breathe, our lungs absorb oxygen from the air. When a fish breathes, oxygen is taken out of the water as it passes through the gills.

The three fins on the cod's back are called dorsal fins. The two fins below its body and near the tail are the ventral fins. There are also two other pairs of fins below its body. These are called the pelvic and the pectoral fins.

Dorsal fins

As the fish swims, it uses its dorsal, ventral, and tail fins to push against the water and move itself forward. It uses the pectoral and pelvic fins to help change direction.

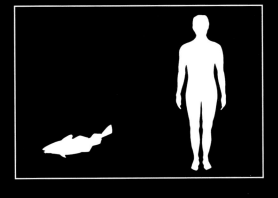

▲ A full-grown Atlantic cod is a big fish. It usually weighs about 25 pounds and is four feet long. Larger cod are rare nowadays, but fishermen sometimes see six-foot giants.

Tail fin

Ventral fins

FIERCE FISH

The cod is a fast-swimming hunter that lives in the northern Atlantic Ocean. It feeds on other fish and sea creatures such as crabs and starfish, which it catches in its sharp teeth. People like to eat cod. They catch millions of these fish every year.

FROG

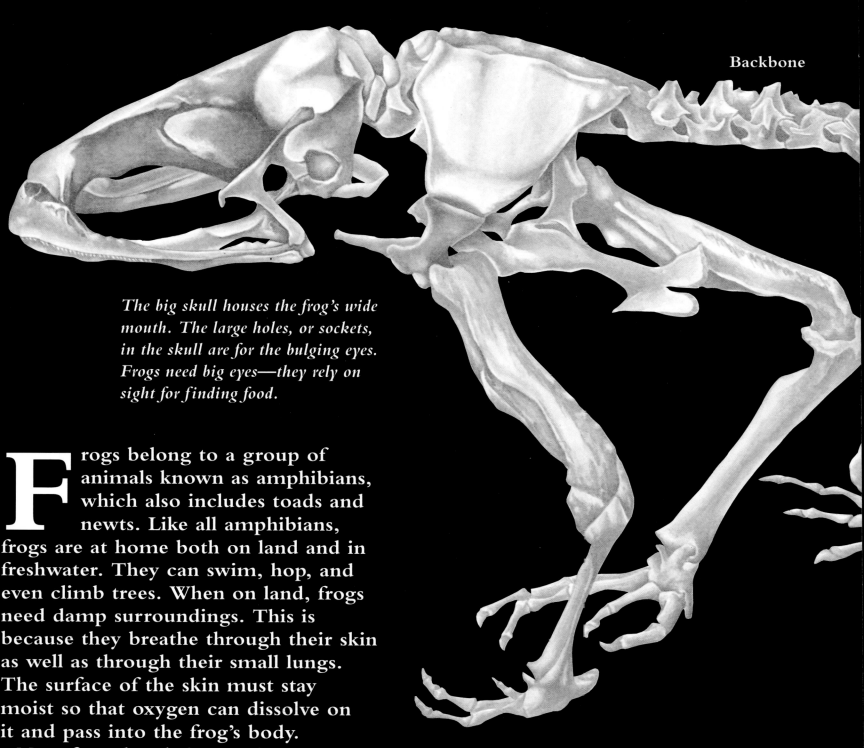

Backbone

The big skull houses the frog's wide mouth. The large holes, or sockets, in the skull are for the bulging eyes. Frogs need big eyes—they rely on sight for finding food.

Foot bones

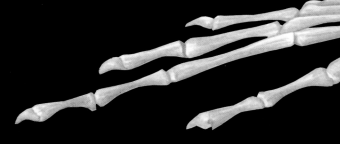

Frogs belong to a group of animals known as amphibians, which also includes toads and newts. Like all amphibians, frogs are at home both on land and in freshwater. They can swim, hop, and even climb trees. When on land, frogs need damp surroundings. This is because they breathe through their skin as well as through their small lungs. The surface of the skin must stay moist so that oxygen can dissolve on it and pass into the frog's body.

Most frogs lay their eggs in water. The eggs hatch into swimming tadpoles that breathe through feathery gills at the sides of the head. As a tadpole matures, it loses its tail and gills and grows legs. About 16 weeks after hatching, the tadpole has become a tiny frog. At the top of the page, you can see how an egg changes into a leaping frog.

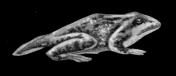  

Look at what a short backbone a frog
has compared to a fish on page 4. This
short spine helps to keep the frog's back
rigid for jumping. The extra-long
hip bones help provide power
for the jump. The frog
has no ribs attached
to its backbone.

Hip bones

**Thigh
bones**

Calf bones

INSECT EATER

On land, the frog eats slugs, snails, insects,
and spiders. It catches its food with its
long sticky tongue. As long as there is some
water nearby, this frog can live happily in
woodlands, fields, and even gardens.

On land, the frog crouches with its long
legs folded. The foot, calf, and thigh are all
about the same length. As the frog leaps,
its legs unfold to push it into the air.

▶Most frogs are
about four inches
long—they could sit
on the palm of your
hand. When
stretched out, a
frog's back legs are
usually longer than
its body.

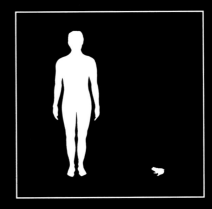

7

Green Turtle

Sea turtles spend most of their lives in the ocean, swimming with the graceful beats of their long, winglike flippers. They must come to the surface to breathe, but they can stay underwater for several hours while resting or sleeping. When turtles do come onto land, they move with difficulty, dragging themselves along with their flippers.

Turtles are reptiles like crocodiles and snakes. The green turtle is one of the biggest of the seven types of sea turtles. Like its land relative, the tortoise, the turtle has a hard shell on its back. This covers its whole body except for head, flippers and tail. The shell is like a suit of armor, protecting the turtle from enemies. The turtle also has a shell on its underside. This is joined to the upper shell at the sides, between the turtle's front and back flippers.

Ocean Traveler

Green turtles live in warm ocean waters throughout the world. The color of the shell varies from animal to animal. It can be olive green, dark brown, or many shades in between. Young green turtles feed on fish and shrimp. Adults eat sea grass. Green turtles are famous for the long journeys they make from their feeding places to the beaches where they lay their eggs. Turtles that live off the coast of South America travel nearly 3,000 miles to lay their eggs on tiny Ascension Island in the Atlantic Ocean.

The turtle's skull is small but strong. All the bones at the top of the head are joined together, making a protective shape like a helmet. The turtle has no teeth. It tears its food apart with its tough jaws.

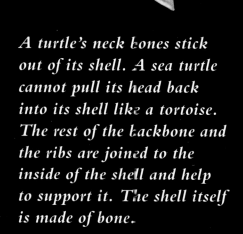

A turtle's neck bones stick out of its shell. A sea turtle cannot pull its head back into its shell like a tortoise. The rest of the backbone and the ribs are joined to the inside of the shell and help to support it. The shell itself is made of bone.

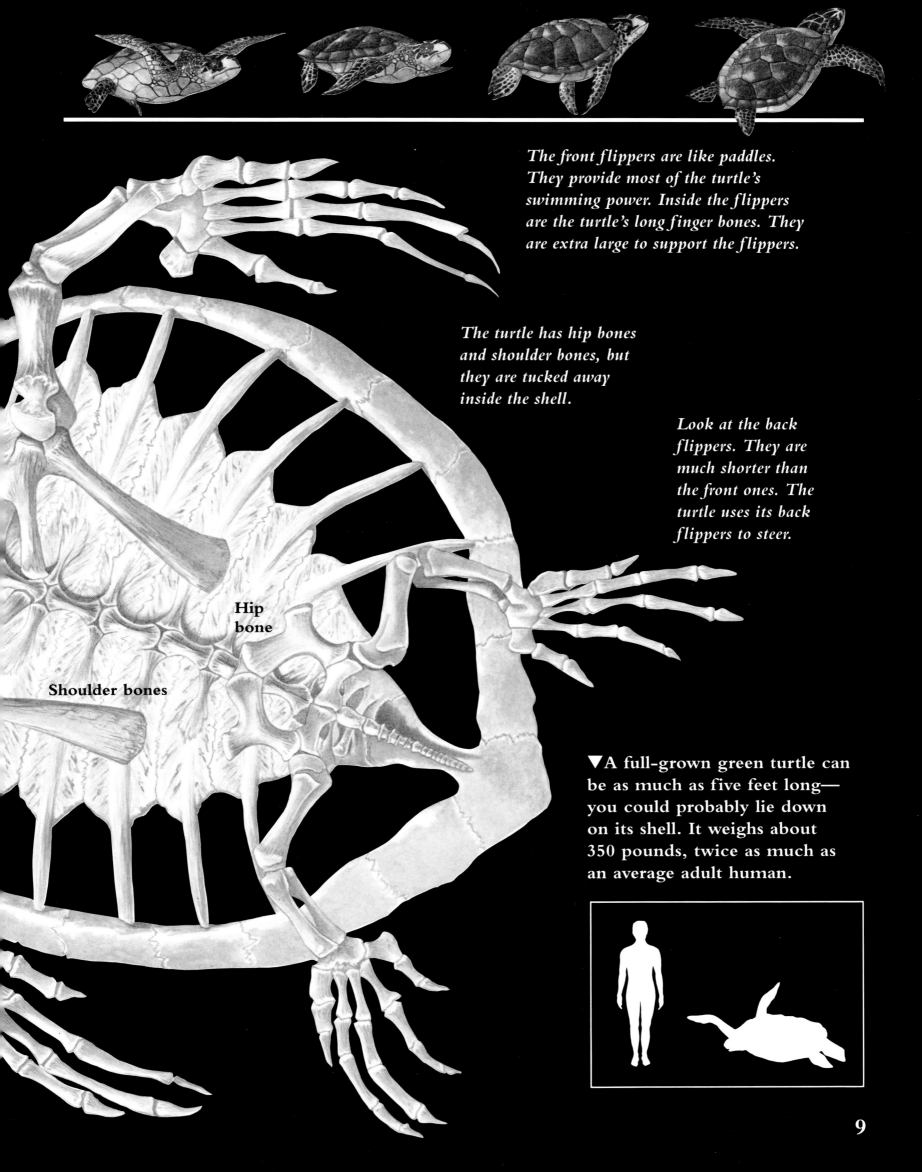

The front flippers are like paddles. They provide most of the turtle's swimming power. Inside the flippers are the turtle's long finger bones. They are extra large to support the flippers.

The turtle has hip bones and shoulder bones, but they are tucked away inside the shell.

Look at the back flippers. They are much shorter than the front ones. The turtle uses its back flippers to steer.

Hip bone

Shoulder bones

▼A full-grown green turtle can be as much as five feet long— you could probably lie down on its shell. It weighs about 350 pounds, twice as much as an average adult human.

NILE CROCODILE

Crocodiles have not changed a great deal since prehistoric times. They still look almost the same as the first crocodiles which lived at the time of the dinosaurs, 200 million years ago. Crocodiles are among the largest of all reptiles. They are related to the alligator, the caiman, and the gavial—a crocodile with a long thin snout.

Crocodiles and alligators are at home both on land and in water and are excellent swimmers. They have long bodies, strong tails, and short legs. An armor of thick scales covers the body and is made even stronger on the back by pieces of bone under the scales.

All crocodiles are meat eaters and hunt for their food. They often lurk half-hidden in a river or waterhole, waiting for prey to come near. With surprising speed, they then seize the victim in their long jaws.

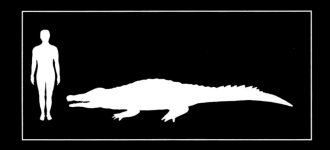

▲ From its nose to the tip of its tail, a Nile crocodile measures about 16 feet—longer than most cars.

Look at the eye sockets at the top of the head and the nostrils at the end of the top jaw. The crocodile's eyes and nose are often all that can be seen as it lies in the water watching for prey.

Nostril

Eye socket

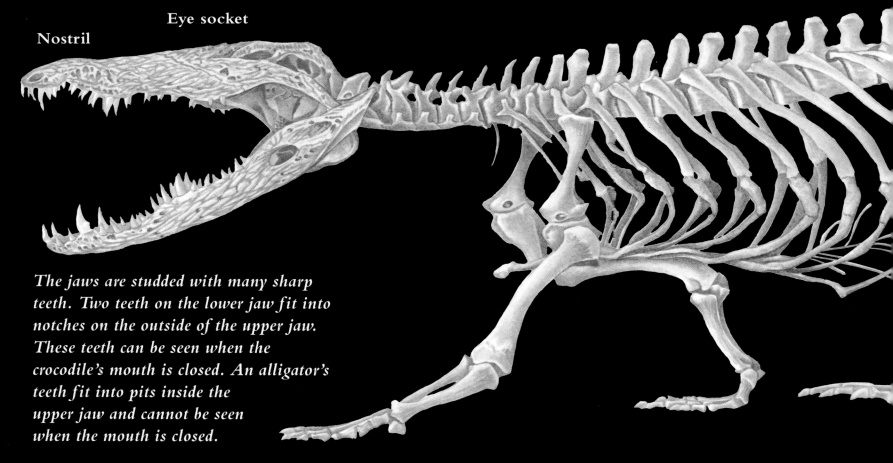

The jaws are studded with many sharp teeth. Two teeth on the lower jaw fit into notches on the outside of the upper jaw. These teeth can be seen when the crocodile's mouth is closed. An alligator's teeth fit into pits inside the upper jaw and cannot be seen when the mouth is closed.

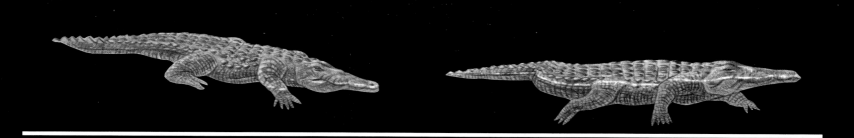

DEADLY AMBUSHER

The Nile crocodile is a fierce hunter. It lives in and alongside rivers, lakes, and waterholes in Africa. Young crocodiles eat small creatures such as insects and frogs. But full-grown crocodiles ambush animals as large as zebra and buffalo.

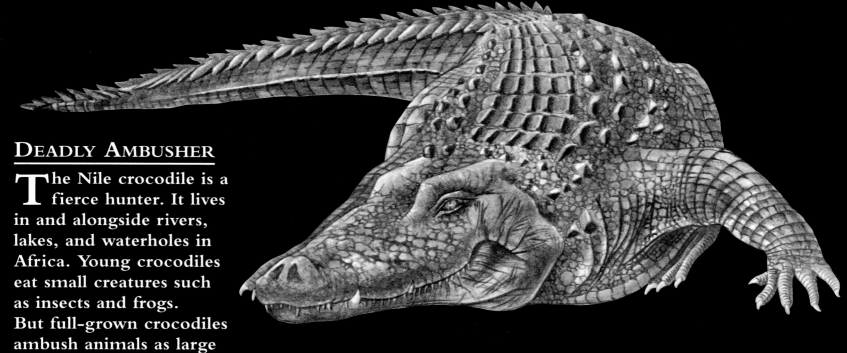

A crocodile can move on land in two ways. It can wriggle along on its belly, pushing itself with its feet (see above). Or it can raise itself off the ground in what is called the "high walk" (see skeleton). A crocodile has five toes on each front foot and four on each back foot.

A long spine and strong tail make the crocodile's body flexible and help it to move in water. The crocodile swims by waving its tail from side to side. As it swims, it holds its legs close to its body. This streamlines the crocodile's shape so that it can move through the water faster.

PIT VIPER

Even though they have no legs, snakes can move fast. Besides wriggling along the ground, most also swim well and can even climb trees. Along with crocodiles and turtles, snakes belong to the group of animals called reptiles. There are more than two thousand types of snakes—from four-inch-long thread snakes to 30-foot pythons. Snakes live in most places in the world except where it is very cold.

All snakes hunt other animals for food. Some, such as the boas, are constrictors. They wrap victims in their strong body coils and squeeze them to death. Others, such as cobras and vipers, have a deadly poisonous bite.

The snake's lightweight skull is made up mostly of jaw bones. This animal can open its mouth very wide because its upper and lower jaws are loosely joined. This allows the snake to swallow large prey.

Vertebrae

NIGHTTIME HUNTER

This dangerous pit viper lives in the forests of Central and South America. It can hunt in the dark with amazing accuracy. On each side of its head is a small pit which is sensitive to heat. When an animal comes near, the snake senses its body heat with these pits and knows just where to strike.

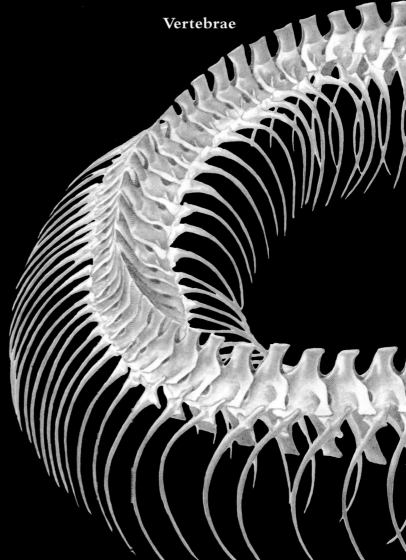

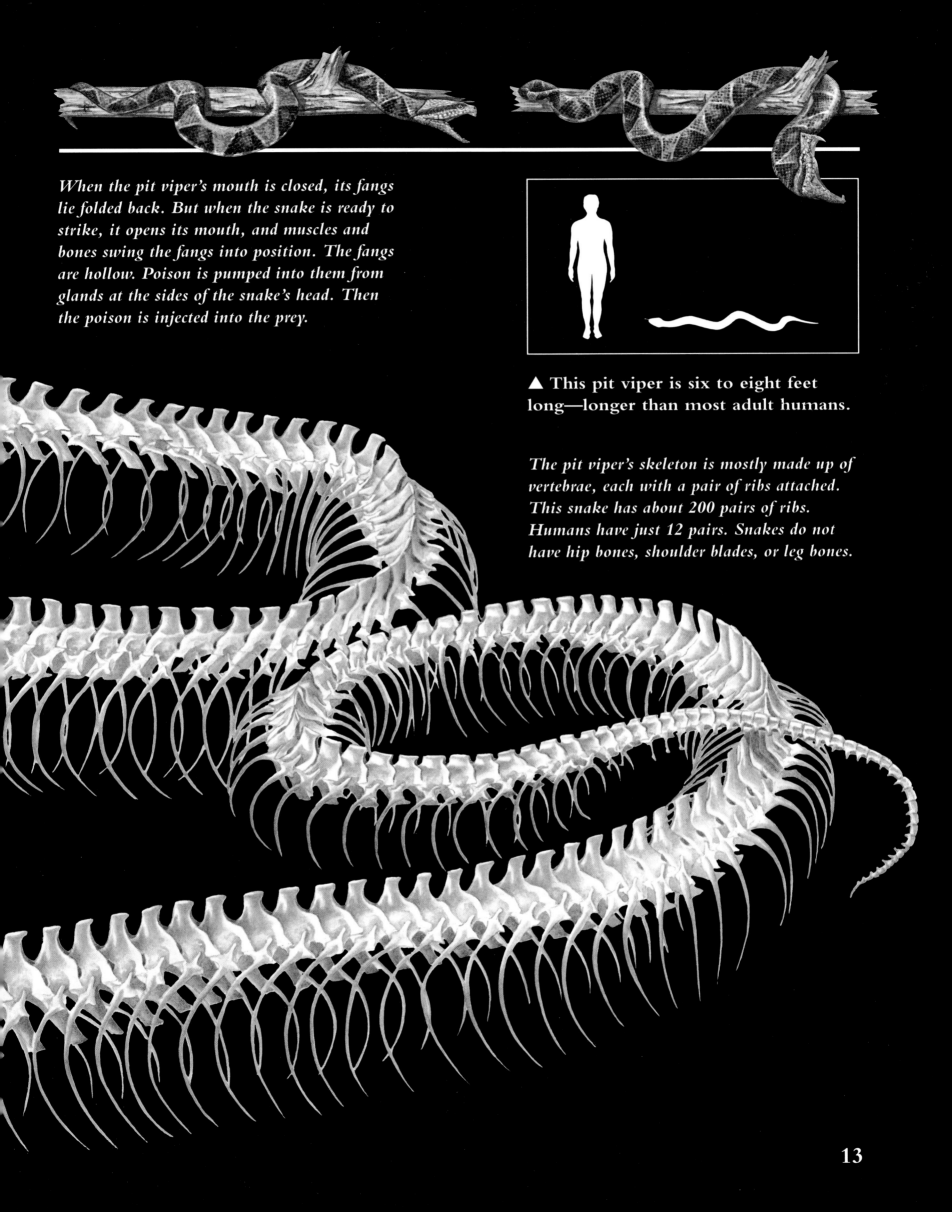

When the pit viper's mouth is closed, its fangs lie folded back. But when the snake is ready to strike, it opens its mouth, and muscles and bones swing the fangs into position. The fangs are hollow. Poison is pumped into them from glands at the sides of the snake's head. Then the poison is injected into the prey.

▲ This pit viper is six to eight feet long—longer than most adult humans.

The pit viper's skeleton is mostly made up of vertebrae, each with a pair of ribs attached. This snake has about 200 pairs of ribs. Humans have just 12 pairs. Snakes do not have hip bones, shoulder blades, or leg bones.

SCARLET MACAW

The skull is light so it does not weigh the bird down in the air. There are large spaces for the macaw's big eyes.

Nostril

Beak

Like all birds, the macaw has no teeth. Instead it has a big hooked beak which covers much of its top and bottom jaws. The beak is made of the same hard material as our finger- and toenails. The two halves of the beak can clamp together to crush food—just like a strong nutcracker.

A bird flaps its wings with the help of large muscles. These are attached to a big, triangular bone called a keel. The keel is part of the bird's sternum (or breastbone).

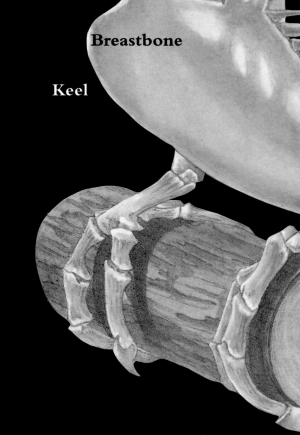

Breastbone

Keel

There are more than 9,000 species of birds in the world. All have feathers, and most can fly. Birds lay eggs which they usually keep warm in nests until their young hatch.

The scarlet macaw is a species of parrot. It is one of the biggest birds in the parrot family, which also includes cockatoos, parakeets, and lovebirds. Parrots are found in the southern half of the world in South America, Africa, Asia, and Australia. They usually live in rain forests or woodlands where they find plenty of fruit, seeds, and nuts to eat. Their strong beaks can crack the hardest shells.

Many kinds of macaws are so beautiful that they have become popular pets. Sadly, this means that some are now very rare in nature. In most countries, it is against the law to take rare birds from the wild to keep as pets.

A bird's bones are not as solid as ours. They are like a honeycomb inside; spaces filled with air keep them light. It would be hard for a bird with heavy bones to fly.

A bird's wing has arm and finger bones similar to those of land animals. But each wing has only three finger bones. The main flying feathers—called the primaries—are attached to the arm bones and the two long finger bones. A third short finger bone supports a "mini-wing" in front of the main wing.
This mini-wing helps control the air flow over the main wing.

SCARLET BEAUTY

With its brilliant red and blue feathers, the scarlet macaw is one of the most striking birds. It usually lives in pairs or families that fly together, searching for nuts and seeds. Scarlet macaws feed quietly but make loud screeching cries when flying. They build nests in holes in tree trunks and lay two or three eggs.

Tail bone

Finger bones

"Mini-wing" bone

Each foot has four toes— two pointing forward, two backward. (Many other birds have three toes pointing forward and one backward.) The macaw's foot is like a clamp—ideal for gripping branches.

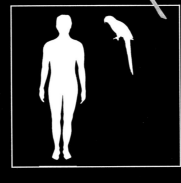

◀ The scarlet macaw is about 33 inches long from its head to the tip of its long tail feathers.

CAPE PENGUIN

U nlike most birds, penguins can't fly. They use their wings like flippers to swim. There are 18 different kinds of penguins. All have mostly black feathers on their backs and white on their stomachs. This coloration helps keep them hidden from enemies in the water.

Penguins live in the oceans of the southern hemisphere, mainly around the icy continent of Antarctica. They spend nearly all of their lives in the sea where they catch fish and squid to eat. The fastest penguin is the gentoo which swims at more than six miles an hour for short distances—faster than the best human swimmers, who are three times its size.

Penguins come onto land to lay their eggs and care for their young. They waddle around upright on their short legs. On ice they sometimes toboggan along, lying flat on their bellies.

The penguin's wings are shaped for swimming instead of flying. They are smaller than the wings of other birds this size and cannot be folded back against the body. The bones are flattened to form a paddlelike shape.

The penguin has more tail bones than the scarlet macaw (see page 14). These bones keep the tail stiff so it can prop the penguin up when it stands on land.

Fourth toe

Front toes

The penguin uses its feet for steering. There are three long front toes, all with strong claws, and a very small fourth toe which is joined to the ankle bone. A web of skin connects the front toes and makes them into more efficient paddles.

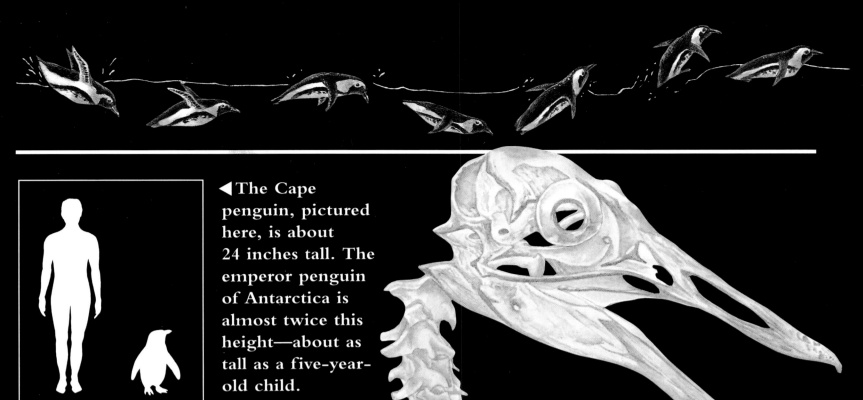

◄ The Cape penguin, pictured here, is about 24 inches tall. The emperor penguin of Antarctica is almost twice this height—about as tall as a five-year-old child.

The penguin's beak is long and pointed—a good shape for catching hold of wriggling fish. Compare the shape of the penguin's beak to the macaw's beak on page 14.

Keel

The keel, part of a bird's breastbone, supports the powerful muscles most birds need to fly. The penguin has a smaller keel than a flying bird. It needs less muscle power to move its flippers for swimming.

Most birds have light bones to help them fly. But the penguin's bones are heavier. The added weight helps the bird dive below the surface of the sea.

UNDERWATER HUNTER

The cool waters off the coasts of southern Africa are the home of the Cape penguin. It can stay underwater for five minutes, catching small fish such as anchovies. On land this penguin gets shelter from the sun by making its nest in a burrow or under rocks.

17

RED KANGAROO

Big and bounding, kangaroos belong to a group of mammals known as marsupials. The word marsupial means pouched animal. Most marsupials have a pouch like a furry pocket in which their young grow and develop. The marsupial baby is born less developed than the babies of other mammals. Immediately after birth, the tiny baby crawls into its mother's pouch. Here it feeds on its mother's milk and grows in safety.

There are more than 250 kinds of marsupials, including marsupial cats and mice, bandicoots, and koalas. Most of these live in Australia and nearby New Guinea, but many kinds of opossums live in North and South America.

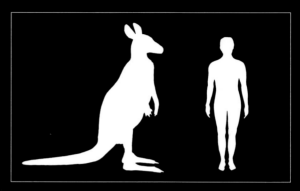

▲ Red kangaroos are the largest kangaroos—and the biggest marsupials. A male stands taller than many adult humans. Its head and body are more than five feet long and its tail measures at least three feet.

DESERT LEAPER

Kangaroos can move on all four legs, but they usually leap along on their strong back legs like the kangaroo at the top of the page. Red kangaroos live in the vast Australian desert and need to travel huge distances to find enough grass and leaves to eat.

When a baby kangaroo is born, it is no bigger than an adult human's thumb. It stays in its mother's pouch until it is over a year old and big enough to find its own food.

A kangaroo's long tail is extremely strong. Look at how big the bones are. Powerful muscles for moving the tail are attached to bones called neural spines. These stick out from the tail bones. The kangaroo uses its tail for balance when it hops. The tail also props up the kangaroo when it stands on its back legs.

Neural spines

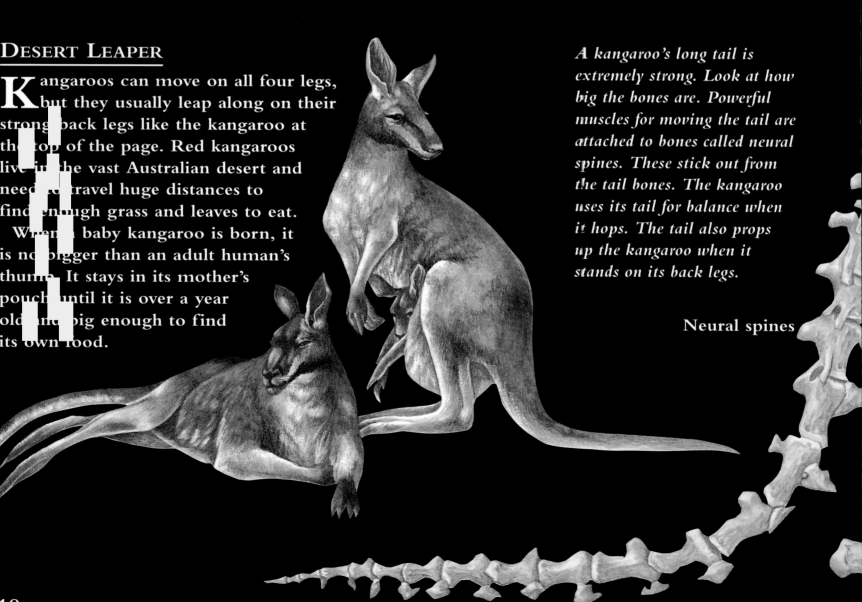

The long backbone is strong but flexible enough to bend and straighten as the kangaroo hops along. Look at the pictures above to see how the backbone moves. The red kangaroo can run at a speed of up to 40 miles an hour. That's a good speed for a car. It can also jump as high as ten feet—twice its own height.

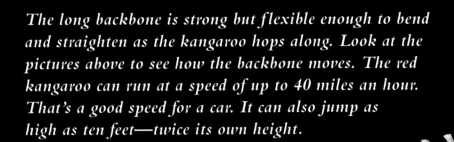

The kangaroo's skull is long and fairly flat on top. The teeth at the front of the long jaws are for chopping off mouthfuls of leaves or grass. Then the tongue moves the food to the teeth farther back in the jaws where it is ground down before swallowing.

Shin bone

The back legs are much longer than the front legs. The shin bone, or tibia, is especially large. The powerful leg muscles are attached to this bone. The large back feet have four toes. The one long toe is used for jumping and walking, and the smaller ones for grooming the fur.

The kangaroo uses its shorter front legs to move on all fours or to hold food. There are sharp claws on the tips of the five long fingers. Rival males fighting over mates sometimes use these claws as weapons when they "box" with one another.

19

FRUIT BAT

Bats take to the sky when night falls. They are mammals like cats, dogs, monkeys, and humans, but bats can fly just as well as birds. They have wings made of thin skin, supported by the long bones of their arms and "hands." The bones are light so the bats are not too heavy to fly. Bats cannot move easily on land. They crawl along, using their back feet and the claws at the tips of their wings.

During the day fruit bats sleep in groups of thousands, hanging upside down in caves or from the branches of trees. Many bats eat insects, but fruit bats eat soft fruits such as figs. Their keen sense of smell helps them find the ripest fruit.

Claw

"Finger" bones

All bats have a claw on their first finger. Fruit bats also have a claw on each second finger. They use their claws to climb in trees and to hold food.

These long bones are the finger bones of the bat's "hands." They help support the wings which stretch down the sides of the body and legs and across to the tips of the fingers. Look at the bird skeleton on page 14, and see how different its wing bones are from those of the bat.

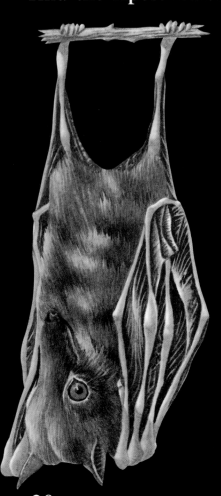

FLYING FOX

There are more than 170 types of fruit bat. They are often called flying foxes because of their foxlike faces. Fruit bats live in tropical places like Southeast Asia and northern Australia where there is always plenty of ripe fruit to feed on. Like all bats, the fruit bat folds its wings close to its sides and hangs by its feet when it rests.

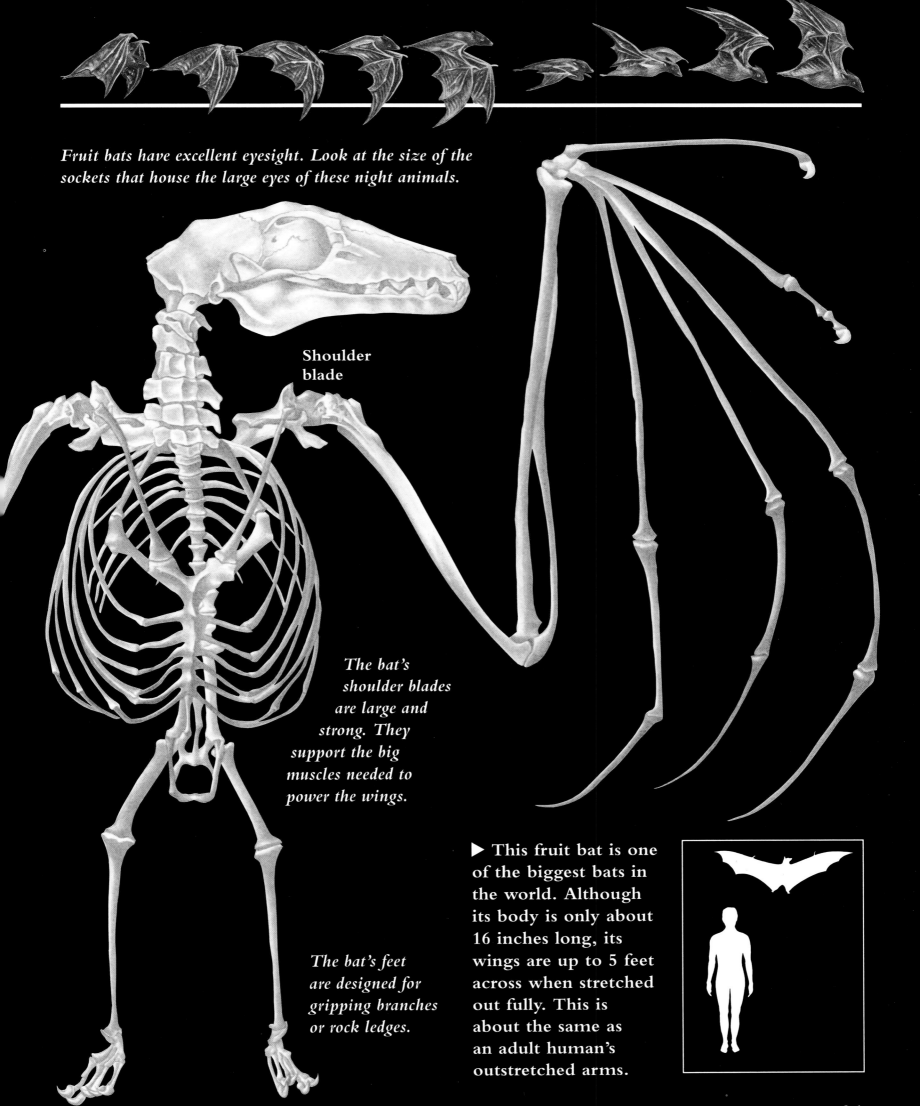

Fruit bats have excellent eyesight. Look at the size of the sockets that house the large eyes of these night animals.

Shoulder
blade

The bat's shoulder blades are large and strong. They support the big muscles needed to power the wings.

The bat's feet are designed for gripping branches or rock ledges.

▶ This fruit bat is one of the biggest bats in the world. Although its body is only about 16 inches long, its wings are up to 5 feet across when stretched out fully. This is about the same as an adult human's outstretched arms.

LION

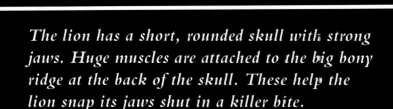

The lion has a short, rounded skull with strong jaws. Huge muscles are attached to the big bony ridge at the back of the skull. These help the lion snap its jaws shut in a killer bite.

The lion kills its prey with the daggerlike teeth, called canines, at the front of its jaws.

The mighty lion with its ferocious roar is actually a big cat. The cat family includes about 37 species, ranging from small wild cats and domestic cats to large, powerful tigers and lions.

Aside from their size, all cats are quite similar. They are hunters that catch other animals with their sharp teeth and claws. They follow their prey quietly or lie in wait. Then they pounce—just like the lion at the top of the page. Lions have excellent eyesight. They see much better in the dark than humans. Their good hearing helps them track down prey.

A male lion has a thick collar of hair called a mane on his neck. It makes him appear larger than he is and more threatening. A female lion is called a lioness and does not have a mane.

The lion has sharp curved claws on its feet. Each claw folds back onto the bone behind it and is protected by the fleshy paw. The claws are kept out of the way when not needed so their points stay sharp.

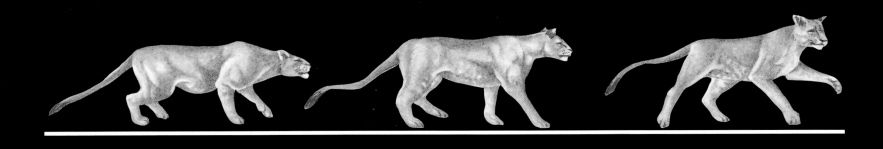

The backbone bends easily so the lion can crouch low and slink along the ground when it stalks its prey.

CARING MOTHER

Most lions live in Africa, but some roam a small area of northern India. Unlike most cats, lions live in families called prides. A pride includes as many as 18 animals, mostly females and young.

Lionesses are good mothers. They care for their cubs for up to two years and teach them how to hunt.

When a lion runs, its long tail swings from side to side. This helps the lion keep its balance.

▼ A full-grown lion is big and heavy. It is eight to ten feet long, and its tail adds another three feet. A male lion weighs about 450 pounds—as much as three human adults. A lioness is slightly smaller and lighter.

Long slender legs help the lion move fast. Lions can run at a speed of more than 35 miles an hour but only for short distances.

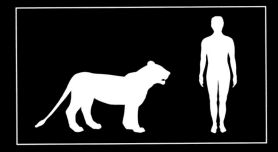

ELEPHANT SEAL

The mighty elephant seal is the biggest of all seals. Its huge body is covered with a thick layer of fatty blubber to protect it from the cold. It weighs as much as a full-grown rhinoceros.

Like sealions and walruses, seals are mammals. They are descended from the same land creatures as cats and dogs but spend most of their time in the sea. Their bodies are torpedo-shaped to suit their watery lives. Instead of legs, they have flippers which they use to move on land and in the sea.

All seals come out of the water to mate and to give birth. Once a year, huge numbers of elephant seals gather together on beaches. Males fight one another to win control of sections of the beach. The winners can mate with the females in their areas. Rival males rear up facing one another; then they crash their great bodies together like the elephant seals at the top of the page. The male elephant seal has a big fleshy snout, which it can puff up when threatening a rival.

The long toe bones of the back feet support the flippers. These flippers provide most of the elephant seal's swimming power.

DEEP DIVER

Elephant seals live along the west coast of North America and around the icy coasts of Antarctica. They can dive down as deep as 1,000 feet to catch fish and squid.

Thigh bone

Lower leg bone

The seal's leg bones are like those of land animals, but they are extremely short and are contained mostly within the body. Compare the short thigh bone, or femur, of the seal to the thigh bone of the horse on page 33.

Toe bones

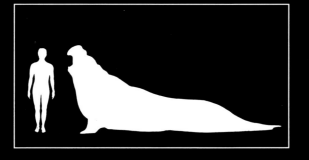

◀ A male elephant seal weighs about 5,000 pounds— more than 30 adult humans. A female weighs less than half as much.

The elephant seal's backbone is very flexible so that the animal can move easily in water. The vertebrae at the end of the backbone are especially big and strong. They support the large muscles needed to move the seal's hind flippers.

At the front of the elephant seal's heavy jaws are sharp pointed teeth called canines. The seal snaps up slippery prey, such as fish, with these. Then it chews its food with the rounded teeth farther back.

Cartilage

The front flippers of the elephant seal contain short, thick leg bones and long finger bones. The seal can prop itself up on these flippers when on land. When swimming, it usually holds these front flippers close to its body so they are out of the way.

Each of the elephant seal's main ribs is divided into two parts. The top part is made of bone, and the bottom part is made of a tough, springy material called cartilage. When the seal dives, the water presses on its chest. The flexible cartilage allows the chest to cave in under this pressure without crushing the ribs.

25

BLUE WHALE

Whales are mammals like cats, dogs, and humans, but they spend their lives swimming in the ocean. They are even born underwater. A whale has a streamlined body like a fish, and flippers instead of legs. Nonetheless, whales need air, so they must come to the water's surface to breathe.

There are two kinds of whales—toothed whales and baleen whales. Toothed whales include killer whales, dolphins, and porpoises. They have sharp teeth and hunt for prey such as fish and penguins. Baleen whales, such as the humpback and the blue whale, are the real giants. Instead of teeth, these whales have huge chunks of a thick, hairy material called baleen hanging from their top jaws. To feed, a baleen whale opens its mouth, and water flows in. Shrimp and other tiny creatures get caught on the baleen, which acts like a sieve. Then the whale swallows the food.

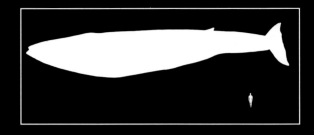

▲ The blue whale is the biggest animal that has ever lived on Earth. It is up to 100 feet long and weighs about 130 tons— more than 80 cars!

The whale has a very short neck, with bones close together. This short neck keeps the body streamlined. If the whale had a long neck, its head would flop around in the water.

The blowhole at the top of the head is the whale's nostril. It allows the whale to breathe without raising its head completely out of the water.

Blowhole

Because the whale's jaw bones are long and curved, there's plenty of room for the bristly baleen.

A whale's front flippers and a land animal's front legs have the same type of main bones. The "fingers" supporting the flippers are long. Most mammals have three bones in each finger. Blue whales have as many as eight.

26

OCEAN GIANT

Blue whales spend some of the year in the icy Arctic and Antarctic oceans where there are plenty of tiny shrimp to eat. In winter they move to warmer waters where the females have their babies. Even a baby blue whale is huge. When it is born, it is about 22 feet long. It would stretch across the floor of a large room. The baby drinks about 150 gallons of its mother's rich milk a day and doubles its weight in a week.

A whale skeleton is surprisingly light. The water supports the whale's weight so its skeleton does not need to be very strong. The skeleton of a land animal of the same size would need to be much heavier.

A whale moves its tail up and down to push itself through the water. Big muscles for moving the tail are attached to the spines sticking out from the tail bones.

Some whales have hip and back leg bones. This means they are related to creatures that walk on land. The blue whale has tiny hip bones that are not joined to the rest of the skeleton.

Tail bones

Hip bones

African Elephant

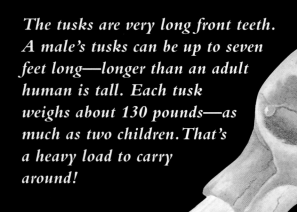

The tusks are very long front teeth. A male's tusks can be up to seven feet long—longer than an adult human is tall. Each tusk weighs about 130 pounds—as much as two children. That's a heavy load to carry around!

Tusks

The skull is large and deep because it has to carry the big tusks and trunk. Huge ridged teeth grow in the strong jaws. Each tooth is about a foot across. At any given time, only two top teeth and two bottom teeth are in use. When a tooth gets too worn from grinding down tough, leafy food, it falls out, and the tooth behind it moves forward.

Elephants are the biggest land animals on Earth today. There are two kinds of elephants—the Asian, which lives in India and Southeast Asia, and the African. Both can survive in most habitats from forest to grassland and swamps. Elephants are friendly animals and live in families. A family includes as many as 20 animals, mostly females and young. Male elephants usually gather in separate herds but stay near the females.

The elephant's trunk is made from its nose and upper lip. The trunk is extremely strong but can make delicate movements such as stroking a newborn calf or sniffing a ripe fruit. With its trunk, the elephant rips branches and leaves from trees and pushes them into its mouth (look at the pictures at the top of the page). The elephant can lift and hold almost anything with its trunk. It also uses it like a huge straw to suck up drinking water—or like a hose for showering.

The thick backbone is unusually straight and inflexible. There are about 20 large ribs. An elephant cannot bend over. It has to kneel down or reach with its trunk.

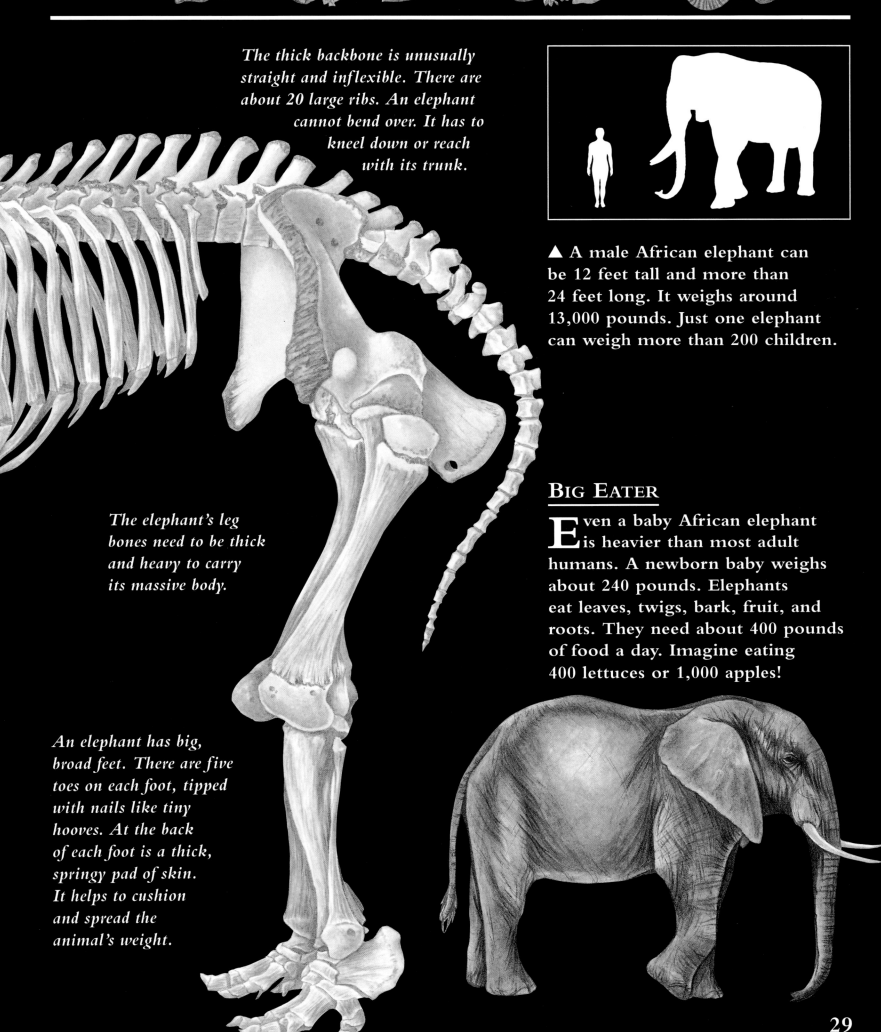

▲ A male African elephant can be 12 feet tall and more than 24 feet long. It weighs around 13,000 pounds. Just one elephant can weigh more than 200 children.

The elephant's leg bones need to be thick and heavy to carry its massive body.

BIG EATER

Even a baby African elephant is heavier than most adult humans. A newborn baby weighs about 240 pounds. Elephants eat leaves, twigs, bark, fruit, and roots. They need about 400 pounds of food a day. Imagine eating 400 lettuces or 1,000 apples!

An elephant has big, broad feet. There are five toes on each foot, tipped with nails like tiny hooves. At the back of each foot is a thick, springy pad of skin. It helps to cushion and spread the animal's weight.

29

MOOSE

Antlers

The bones sticking up from the backbone are called neural spines. They are attached to powerful muscles. These muscles stretch to the back of the heavy head and help to support it.

Neural spines

Antlers are made of bone and grow from the top of the skull. Each winter, after the mating season, the moose's antlers drop off. A new pair grows with more branches than those of the year before. Antlers grow fast—more than half an inch a day.

Outside toes

With its huge, spreading antlers and humped shoulders, the moose is an awesome creature. It is the largest member of the deer family. There are more than 30 kinds of deer, including the caribou (or reindeer), the white-tailed deer, and the tiny musk deer which weighs only 20 pounds.

Most male deer have antlers. Females, except for female caribou, do not. Male deer use their antlers in fierce battles with rival males to win mates. They push each other back and forth, snorting and grunting, until one of them gives in and goes away—as is shown at the top of the page.

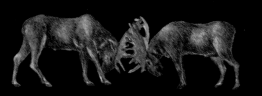

WOODLAND DWELLER

Moose live in wooded areas in North America. In summer they eat mostly the waterweeds in ponds. In winter they feed on twigs and tree bark.

Trees are useful to moose in another way. When new antlers first grow in, they are covered with soft skin called velvet. This skin carries blood to the growing antlers. Once the antlers are full grown, the velvet starts to fall off. The moose rubs its antlers against a tree to remove the last shreds. Otherwise the velvet might get in the moose's way when it fights.

Knee

Ankle

Middle toes

The moose walks around on its toes. Just look at where its ankles are! The bones below the ankle look like part of the leg, but they are actually long foot bones.

Like all deer, the moose has four toes on each foot. The ancestors of the moose walked with all four toes on the ground. But as the moose evolved, its feet changed to help make it a fast runner. The two large middle toes form the hoof that the moose walks on. The two outside toes are much smaller and are no longer used for walking.

▼ A male moose is more than eight feet long and stands up to six feet high at the shoulder. With its mighty antlers, it towers over humans. Female moose are smaller—about three-quarters the size of males.

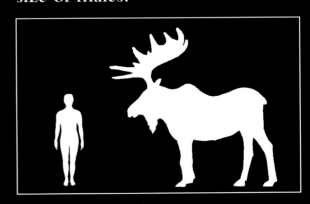

31

HORSE

For more than five thousand years, horses have worked for humans. Before cars and trains were invented, horses were a main form of transportation. They carried loads and people and pulled farm equipment. There are still working horses on farms and ranches, and millions are also used for racing, riding, and other sports.

Horses belong to the group of mammals that also includes donkeys and zebras. Tame (or domestic) horses are found all over the world. Today the only true wild species is the Przewalski's horse of Asia.

Horses have four different ways of moving—walking, trotting, cantering, and, fastest of all, galloping. The horse at the top of the page is galloping. At one stage of the gallop, all four feet are off the ground.

The horse has a long narrow skull. The many teeth it needs for chewing grass can fit inside its big jaws. Look at how large the nostril area is. Horses have a very good sense of smell.

The big teeth at the front of the jaws are called incisors. The horse uses these to chop off mouthfuls of grass. Then the horse chews up its food with the molar teeth farther back.

GRASS EATER

Domestic horses like this one often work hard, carrying loads or racing. They are given plenty of different grains, such as oats and barley, to eat— as well as grass and hay. In the wild, horses eat grass and other small plants. They spend most of their day feeding.

Bones called neural spines stick up from the horse's backbone. Strong muscles to lift the heavy head and neck are attached to these. The big rib cage protects the lungs. A horse has large lungs so that it can take in lots of air as it runs fast.

▶ The average domestic horse stands between five and six feet high from hoof to shoulder—taller than most humans. It weighs about 1,300 pounds—as much as eight or nine adult humans.

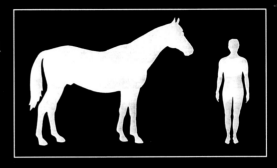

The horse can flick its tail over its back to brush away irritating insects. The muscles that move the tail are attached to the spines at the top of the tail.

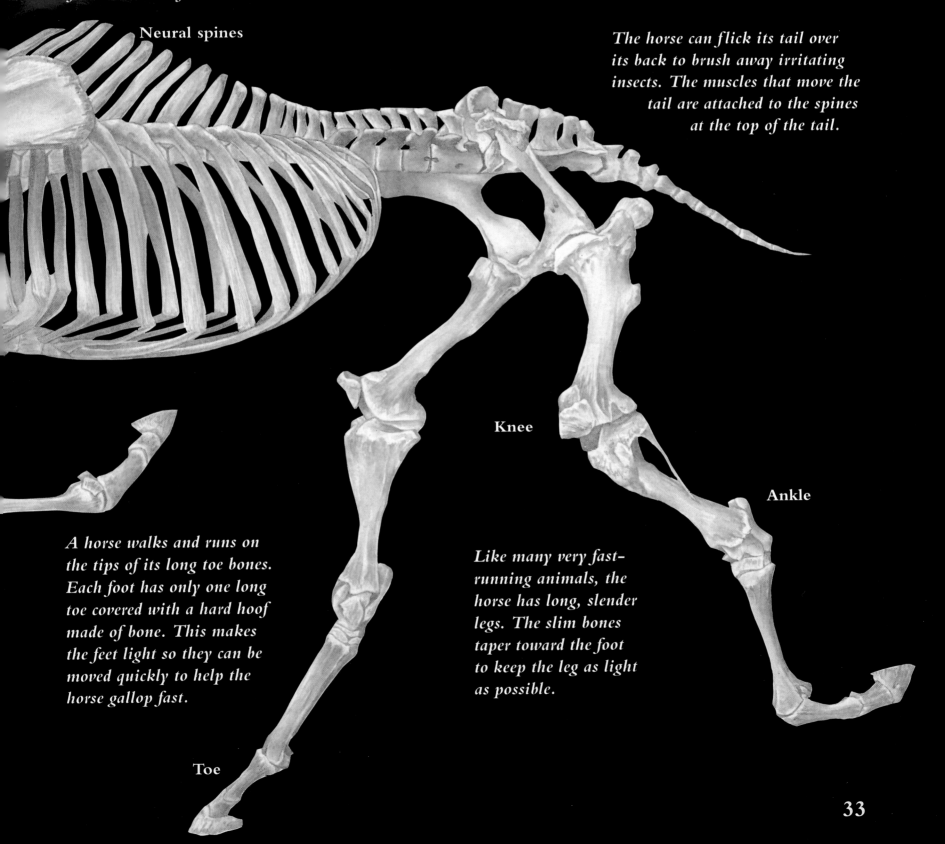

Neural spines

Knee

Ankle

A horse walks and runs on the tips of its long toe bones. Each foot has only one long toe covered with a hard hoof made of bone. This makes the feet light so they can be moved quickly to help the horse gallop fast.

Like many very fast-running animals, the horse has long, slender legs. The slim bones taper toward the foot to keep the leg as light as possible.

Toe

33

THREE-TOED SLOTH

Sloths are famous for moving slowly. One mother sloth "hurrying" to her baby took an hour to travel 15 feet! These strange mammals spend much of their lives hanging upside down in trees in South American rain forests. They rarely come down to the ground. Sloths have become so adapted to their upside-down life that they can no longer stand upright on land. They can only drag themselves along with their long front legs. But sloths are good swimmers and can move easily in jungle rivers.

There are two different types of sloths— three-toed and two-toed. All sloths have three toes on their back feet, but two-toed sloths have only two on their front feet. Sloths feed mostly on leaves. Their sight is poor, so they find their food by smell and touch. A sloth's stomach works as slowly as its legs. It can take up to a month to digest a meal.

The sloth's front legs are much longer than its back legs. It uses its front legs to pull itself along as it moves from branch to branch in the trees.

The three-toed sloth has nine neck bones. Most other mammals have only six or seven. Extra bones make the sloth's neck flexible. The sloth can turn its head around completely to look down at the ground.

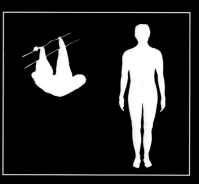

◀ The three-toed sloth is about two feet long including its short tail. It weighs about nine or ten pounds—not much more than a large domestic cat.

The sloth's skull is short and rounded. It has 16 to 20 teeth which get worn down from chewing tough leaves.

A strong claw—about three inches long—tips each toe. These claws are like hooks which the sloth uses to hang onto branches. The sloth clings so tightly that it can even sleep upside down!

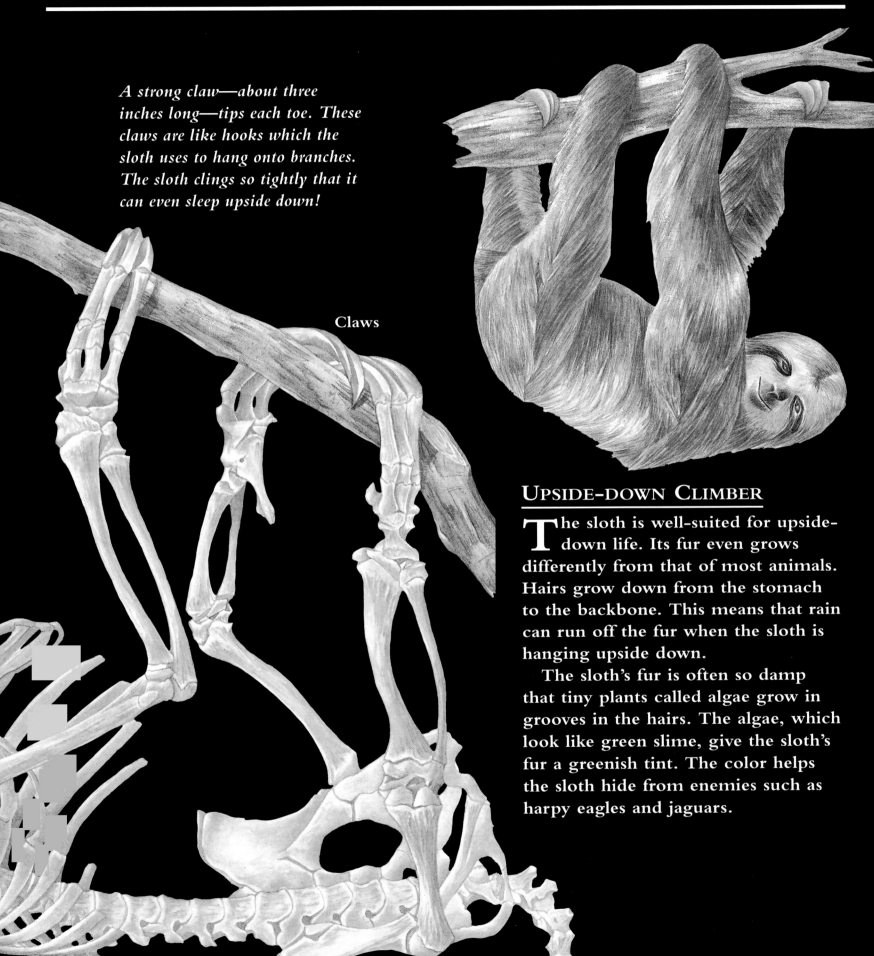

Claws

UPSIDE-DOWN CLIMBER

The sloth is well-suited for upside-down life. Its fur even grows differently from that of most animals. Hairs grow down from the stomach to the backbone. This means that rain can run off the fur when the sloth is hanging upside down.

The sloth's fur is often so damp that tiny plants called algae grow in grooves in the hairs. The algae, which look like green slime, give the sloth's fur a greenish tint. The color helps the sloth hide from enemies such as harpy eagles and jaguars.

GORILLA

Gorillas may look fierce, but these great apes are usually peaceful, gentle creatures. They belong to the group of mammals known as primates that also includes chimpanzees and humans.

Gorillas live in dense tropical rain forests in central and west Africa. They spend most of the day feeding on plants such as bamboo, thistles, and vines. Some gorillas also eat insects, slugs, and snails. At night they curl up in nests made of branches and leaves up in the trees or down on the ground.

Gorillas can walk on two legs, but they usually move around on all fours. They are good climbers. Gorillas rarely fight, but if two dominant males meet, or if a young male intrudes on another male's family, they often rear up, beat their chests, and roar to threaten one another.

FAMILY DWELLER

Gorillas live in families made up of mothers and young led by an older male. Most families have ten or twelve members, but some have up to 30. The male leaders are called silverbacks because silvery white hair grows on their backs after the age of ten or so. Young males live alone for some years after leaving their parents and before they have their own families.

The front of the gorilla's skull comes forward to form a snout. It is not flat like a human face. A bony ridge on the forehead helps protect the eyes from injury.

The gorilla's arms are longer than its legs. When it moves on all fours, the gorilla leans on the knuckles of its hands.

Knuckles

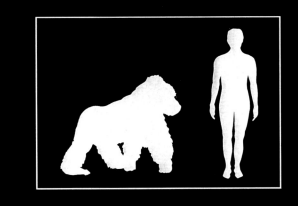

▲ A male gorilla stands about six feet tall—the same height as a tall man, but a gorilla weighs much more. A full-grown male can weigh 600 pounds—as much as four humans. Female gorillas are smaller. They usually stand about five feet tall and weigh less than half the average male.

Thigh bone

A gorilla's upper and lower leg bones form a straight line. The thigh bones do not slant in toward the knees as they do in humans (look at page 38). This makes the gorilla less steady on two legs than a human. When a gorilla walks upright, it can only waddle along.

The gorilla's foot is well designed to grasp objects and hold onto branches. Its big toe does not lie in a row with the other toes. Instead it is separate like the thumb of a human hand. A gorilla's big toe can touch each of the other toes on the same foot—just the way a human's thumb can touch each finger on the same hand.

Big toe

HUMAN

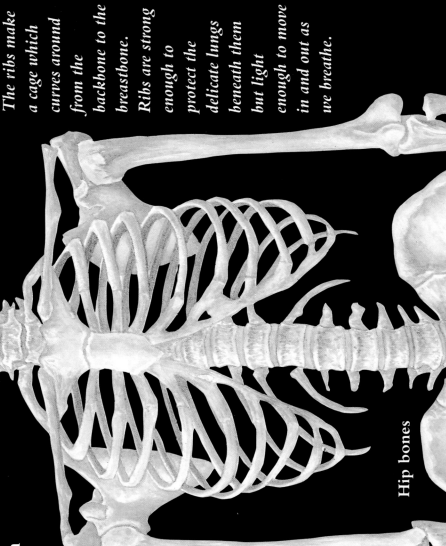

Scientists believe that the first humans evolved about two million years ago. Today there are more than five billion humans, and we rule life on Earth. But we have a long way to go to beat the dinosaurs' record. They were the dominant animals on the planet for more than 130 million years.

Walking on two legs helped the early humans succeed as a species. Their hands and arms were free for handling food and tools. Standing humans were also higher off the ground and better able to see and hear the approach of something dangerous. The size of the human brain helped, too. It is much bigger than a gorilla's or a chimpanzee's.

An adult human's body contains 206 bones. Surprisingly, a newborn baby has many more—about 350 bones! As a baby grows, some bones join together to make larger ones.

The human backbone is made up of many small bones called vertebrae—just like the backbones of other animals. But the human backbone is a vertical support. In four-legged animals, it is a horizontal support. At the end of the backbone is the coccyx or tail bone. This is all the tail that humans have left.

The top of the skull is large and round. It holds and protects the big brain. Although most of the skull looks like one big bone, it is made of 22 bones joined tightly together. Special hinges connect the lower jaw to the rest of the skull so the jaw moves easily.

The ribs make a cage which curves around from the backbone to the breastbone. Ribs are strong enough to protect the delicate lungs beneath them but light enough to move in and out as we breathe.

Hip bones

Coccyx

The 27 bones of a human hand make for great flexibility. Fingers and thumb can touch together which helps us grasp even the smallest objects firmly.

The human foot is a flat platform designed for walking—not for gripping branches. Human toes are much shorter than gorilla toes, and our big toe cannot be placed against our other toes. We have 26 bones in each foot.

The thigh bone, or femur, is the largest bone in the human body. The thigh bones are angled so that they place the lower limbs directly under the body's weight. This makes walking on two legs easier.

The hip bones, or pelvis, connect the legs to the torso. Animals that walk mostly on four legs have long pelvises. Humans have a more bowl-shaped pelvis, suited to upright movement on two legs, with the legs placed directly below the torso.

Versatile Mover

Humans cannot run as fast as horses, jump as high as kangaroos, or swim as gracefully as seals. But we do all these things pretty well. While the bodies of many other animals are specialized for a particular way of life, humans are built for a remarkable variety of activity.

DINOSAURS

KEY
Ocean
Land
Shallow sea

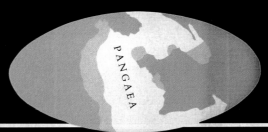

In the Triassic period much of the world's land was joined together. This supercontinent was known as Pangaea.

Millions of years ago, dinosaurs and other reptiles such as ichthyosaurs, plesiosaurs, and pterosaurs dominated life on earth. They lived from late Triassic times to the end of the Cretaceous, about 64 million years ago.

The top chart here shows the dinosaurs in relation to other types of animals. It shows, for example, how birds are believed to be related to dinosaurs. The lower chart shows the two groups of dinosaurs in more detail and the links among the dinosaurs shown in this book.

At the time of the dinosaurs, the world did not look as it does now. The continents, once all joined in one land mass, were slowly drifting apart. The maps at the top of the page show the changing shape of the dinosaurs' world.

PERMIAN 280–225 m.y.a.	TRIASSIC 225–195 m.y.a.

Note: m.y.a. means "million years ago."

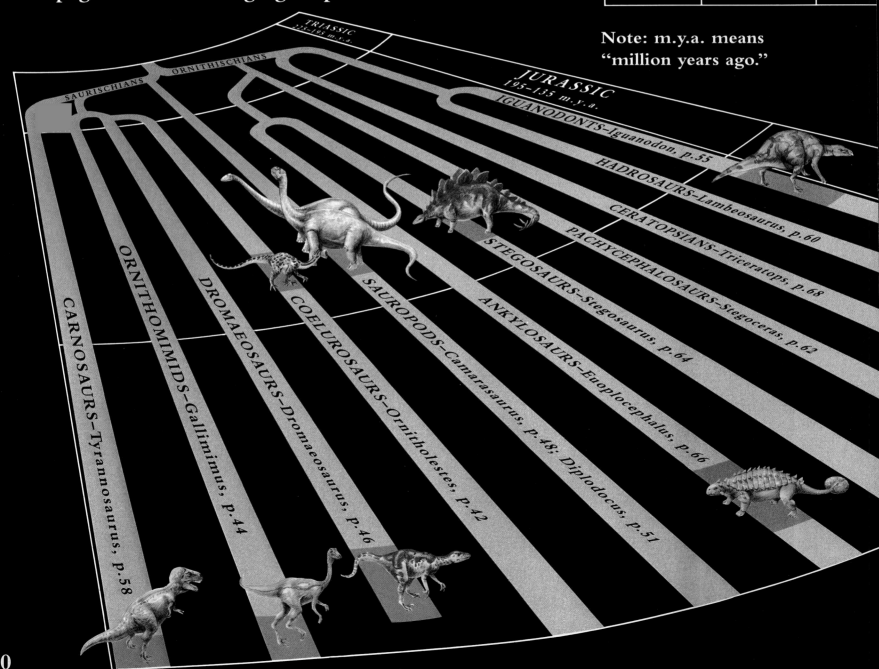

In the early Cretaceous period North America split from South America and a sea separated Europe from Asia.

By the late Cretaceous period continents had drifted farther apart. North America was divided in two by a sea.

URASSIC 95-135 m.y.a.	CRETACEOUS 135-64 m.y.a.	CENOZOIC 64 m.y.a.–present day
		TORTOISES/TURTLES →
		MAMMALS →
ICHTHYOSAURS–Ophthalmosaurus, p.70		
PLESIOSAURS–Cryptoclidus, p.72		
		LIZARDS →
		SNAKES →
		CROCODILES →
PTEROSAURS–Anhanguera, p.74		
ORNITHISCHIAN DINOSAURS	} SEE DETAILED CHART BELOW	
SAURISCHIAN DINOSAURS		
BIRDS–Archaeopteryx p.76		

At the end of the Cretaceous period, 64 million years ago, all dinosaurs, ichthyosaurs, plesiosaurs, and pterosaurs had died out. No one knows why this extraordinary mass extinction occurred, but many experts think that a giant meteorite hit the earth at this time. The huge amount of rock thrown into the atmosphere by the impact would have changed the earth's climate for many years. Some types of animals, such as dinosaurs, would have been unable to survive this change.

The animals on the charts are those featured in the following pages. The darker colored areas on the bars show the period during which each type of animal probably existed.

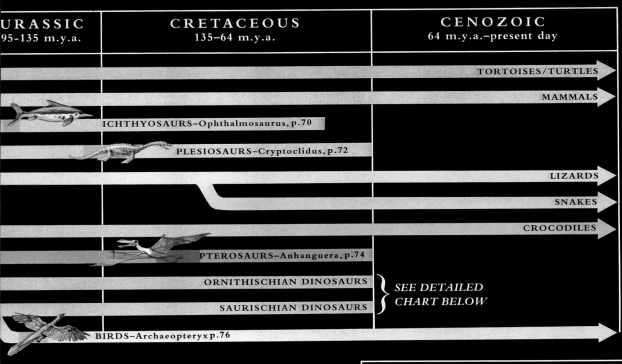

CRETACEOUS 135-64 m.y.a.

Ornithischian dinosaur *Iguanodon*

Ischium
Pubis

Saurischian dinosaur *Ornitholestes*

Ischium
Pubis

Both groups of dinosaurs included several families. Each family contained many different types of dinosaurs. For example, the hadrosaur family in the ornithischian group included the dinosaur *Lambeosaurus* and about 16 other known species.

DINOSAUR HIPS

There were two groups of dinosaurs: ornithischians and saurischians. The main differences between them lay in the hip bones. In saurischians, the pubis bone points away from the ischium bone. In ornithischians, part of the pubis runs below the ischium (see pictures).

ORNITHOLESTES

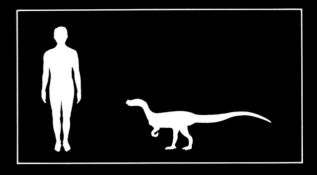

A small, lightly built dinosaur with a whiplike tail, *Ornitholestes* was a fast-moving hunter that caught prey in its slender, clawed hands. The pictures across the top here show how *Ornitholestes* chased and caught creatures such as lizards and frogs. It may also have scavenged food from the kills of larger dinosaurs.

Ornitholestes belonged to the coelurosaur group of dinosaurs, which were lightweight hunters. The name *coelurosaur* means "hollow-tailed lizard." It refers to the thin-walled, hollow bones that made up the tails of these dinosaurs and much of their slender bodies. *Ornitholestes* looked birdlike, and many scientists think birds may have evolved from dinosaurs similar to this one.

▲ *Ornitholestes* was only six feet long from nose to tail tip. It weighed 28 pounds—about the weight of a small dog.

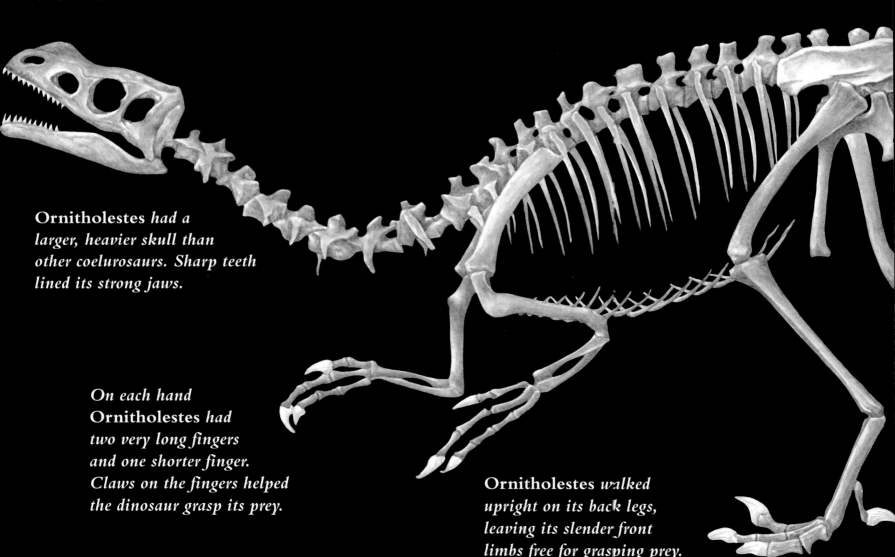

Ornitholestes *had a larger, heavier skull than other coelurosaurs. Sharp teeth lined its strong jaws.*

On each hand Ornitholestes *had two very long fingers and one shorter finger. Claws on the fingers helped the dinosaur grasp its prey.*

Ornitholestes *walked upright on its back legs, leaving its slender front limbs free for grasping prey.*

Scientists once thought that **Ornitholestes** *dragged its tail along the ground. Now most scientists believe that the dinosaur held its tail high to balance the front of the body as it ran.*

The long, slender tail of **Ornitholestes** *made up more than half its length.*

The structure of the back legs shows that **Ornitholestes** *was a fast runner. The bones were light, and the ankle and toe bones long and slender.*

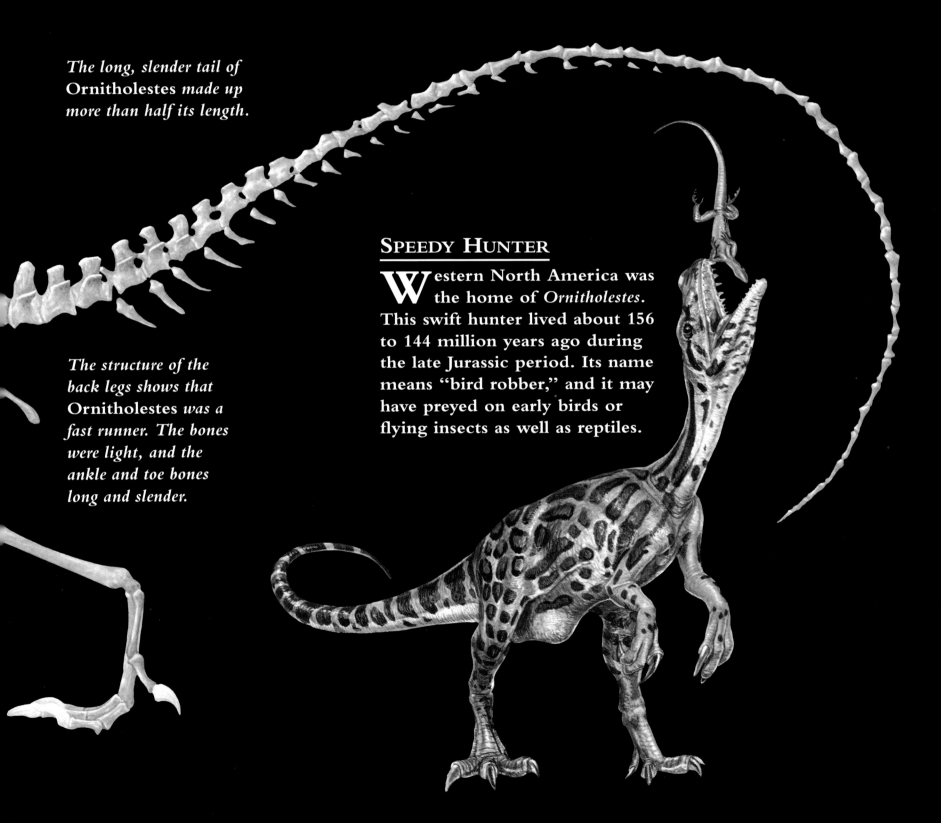

SPEEDY HUNTER

Western North America was the home of *Ornitholestes.* This swift hunter lived about 156 to 144 million years ago during the late Jurassic period. Its name means "bird robber," and it may have preyed on early birds or flying insects as well as reptiles.

GALLIMIMUS

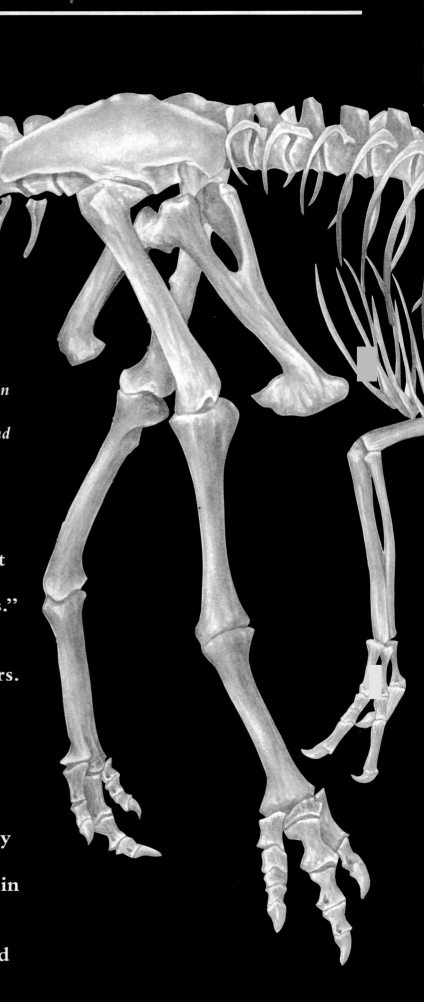

When running, Gallimimus held its long tail straight out. This helped balance its head and neck. (See the pictures in the top panel.)

Gallimimus moved upright on its two long back legs. Its feet, with their long upper bones and three slim toes, were ideally suited for running.

Fast-running *Gallimimus* was the largest of a group of dinosaurs known as ornithomimids, or "ostrich dinosaurs." With their slender legs, long, slim necks, and small heads, they looked like the ostriches of today, which are also swift runners.

Ornithomimids lived in Asia and North America and were intelligent, keen-sighted hunters. Scientists believe that the fastest "ostrich dinosaurs" could sprint at up to 40 miles an hour. In groups, they sped across open plains searching for prey. They also dug into the ground to find and eat eggs buried by other dinosaurs.

Speed was the ornithomimids' best defense in the face of danger. They did not have strong teeth or big claws to protect themselves from larger attackers, but few other dinosaurs could catch them when running at full speed.

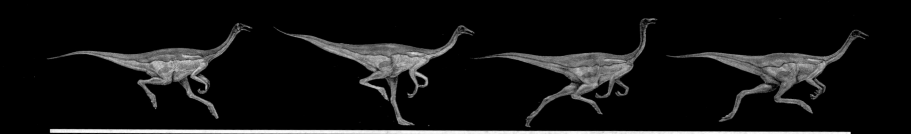

The long, flexible neck of Gallimimus supported a small, light head. Its long, narrow jaws gave this dinosaur a birdlike look. Because it had no teeth, Gallimimus swallowed its food whole.

Look at the big eye sockets. These held the large eyes that helped Gallimimus to spot prey—and danger. The ring of bony plates within the eye socket helped keep the shape of the eye.

Gallimimus *had slender hands, each with three sharp claws. It used these claws to capture and hold on to prey.*

▼ Nearly 17 feet long, *Gallimimus* was almost twice the size of a modern ostrich. The dinosaur weighed about 340 pounds—more than two adult people.

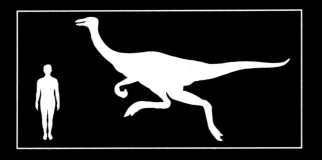

FAST MOVER

About 70 million years ago, *Gallimimus* lived in eastern Asia, in what is now Mongolia. This late Cretaceous dinosaur caught and ate insects and other small creatures such as lizards and frogs. It also pulled down the branches of trees with its long, clawed fingers and fed on leaves, buds, and fruits.

DROMAEOSAURUS

One of the fiercest hunters of its time, *Dromaeosaurus* was a slender, agile, two-legged dinosaur, built for fast movement. Many scientists believe that *Dromaeosaurus*, when running on two legs, could have reached a speed of almost 40 miles an hour. *Dromaeosaurus* lived in North America and belonged to the dromaeosaurid family. Other members of the family lived in Europe and Asia.

Dromaeosaurus was no larger than many other hunting dinosaurs of the time, but it had a special weapon—a large claw on the second toe of each foot. When hunting, the dinosaur chased its prey, then leapt off the ground to tear at the victim with these claws. (Look at the pictures at the top of the page to see *Dromaeosaurus* in action.)

The long tail was strengthened by bony rods growing backward from each of the tail bones. Muscles attached to these bony rods kept the tail stiff and still. This tail helped balance the dinosaur's body as it ran or attacked prey.

SPEEDY HUNTER

Dromaeosaurus lived in the late Cretaceous period, 76 to 70 million years ago. It had a large brain and was intelligent. Hunting in packs, dromaeosaurs could attack and bring down huge, plant-eating dinosaurs much larger than themselves.

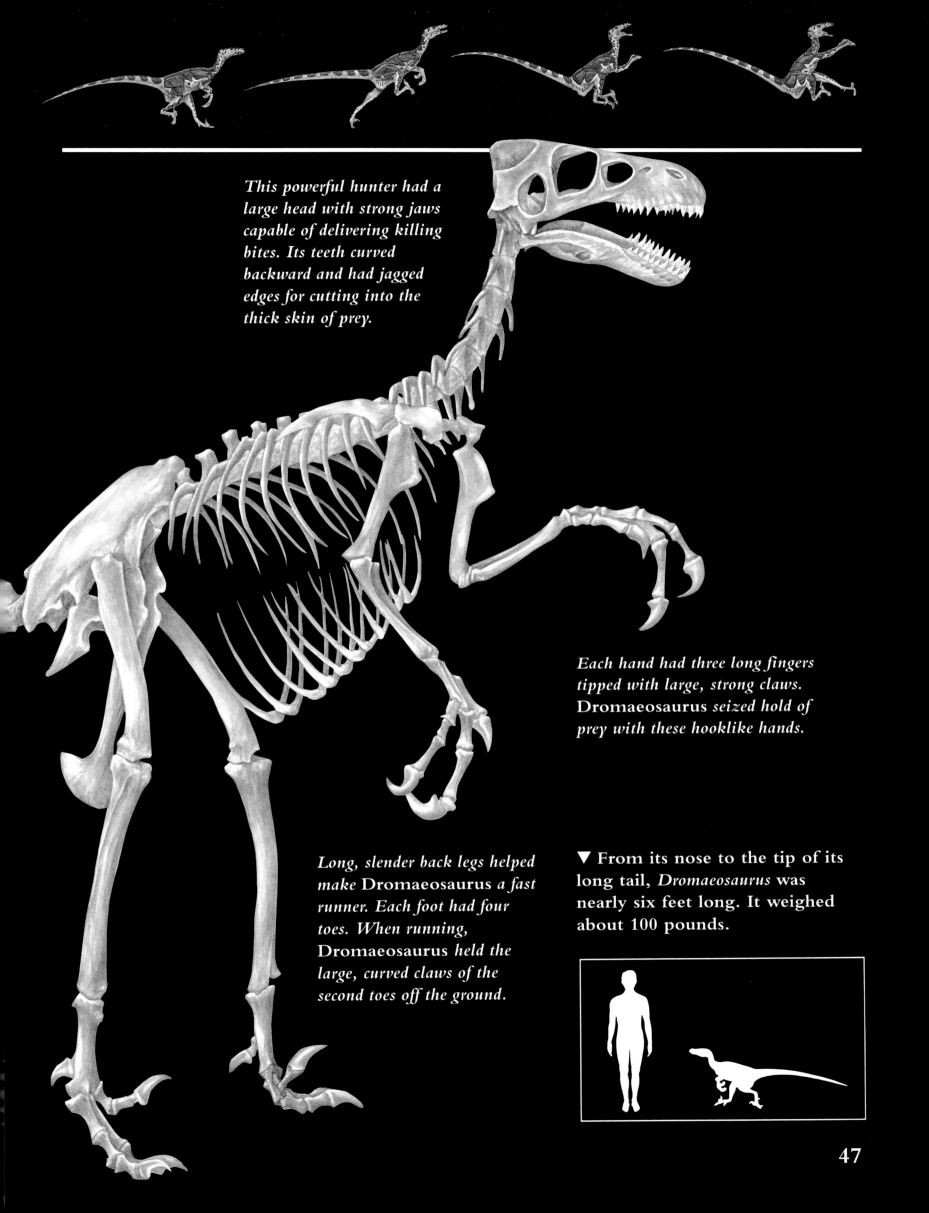

This powerful hunter had a large head with strong jaws capable of delivering killing bites. Its teeth curved backward and had jagged edges for cutting into the thick skin of prey.

Each hand had three long fingers tipped with large, strong claws. *Dromaeosaurus* seized hold of prey with these hooklike hands.

Long, slender back legs helped make **Dromaeosaurus** *a fast runner. Each foot had four toes. When running, Dromaeosaurus held the large, curved claws of the second toes off the ground.*

▼ From its nose to the tip of its long tail, *Dromaeosaurus* was nearly six feet long. It weighed about 100 pounds.

CAMARASAURUS

Grooves in the tops of the neck and back vertebrae carried special long ligaments—bands of tough body tissue that hold bones together. These ligaments helped support the weight of the dinosaur's head and neck.

The skull of Camarasaurus was broad and deep, with large spaces to allow for the nostrils. These were high on the head—perhaps so they did not get blocked with leaves when the dinosaur fed. The jaws were studded with lots of chisel-shaped teeth, which the dinosaur used to strip leaves from branches.

There were twelve vertebrae in the long neck of Camarasaurus, compared to seven in the neck of a giraffe.

Large feet with five toes helped spread the massive weight of this dinosaur. The inside toe on each foot had a large, curved claw. The rest had blunt nails.

A plant-eating giant, mighty *Camarasaurus* belonged to the sauropod group of dinosaurs. Sauropods were the largest of all dinosaurs and the biggest land animals that have ever lived. All had huge bodies, thick pillarlike legs, and long tails and necks. Most sauropods were more than 50 feet long. They were probably not fast movers and relied on their bulk to protect them from attack.

Animals of the size of *Camarasaurus* must have been extremely heavy. Some of the vertebrae and skull bones were hollow, making the skeleton lighter but just as strong.

Camarasaurus had a shorter neck than some other sauropods, such as *Diplodocus* (see pages 51–54), but could still reach up into trees to tear off mouthfuls of leaves. It moved on four legs and did not rear up on its back legs to feed. Just as crocodiles do today, *Camarasaurus* deliberately swallowed stones to help grind up the food in its stomach.

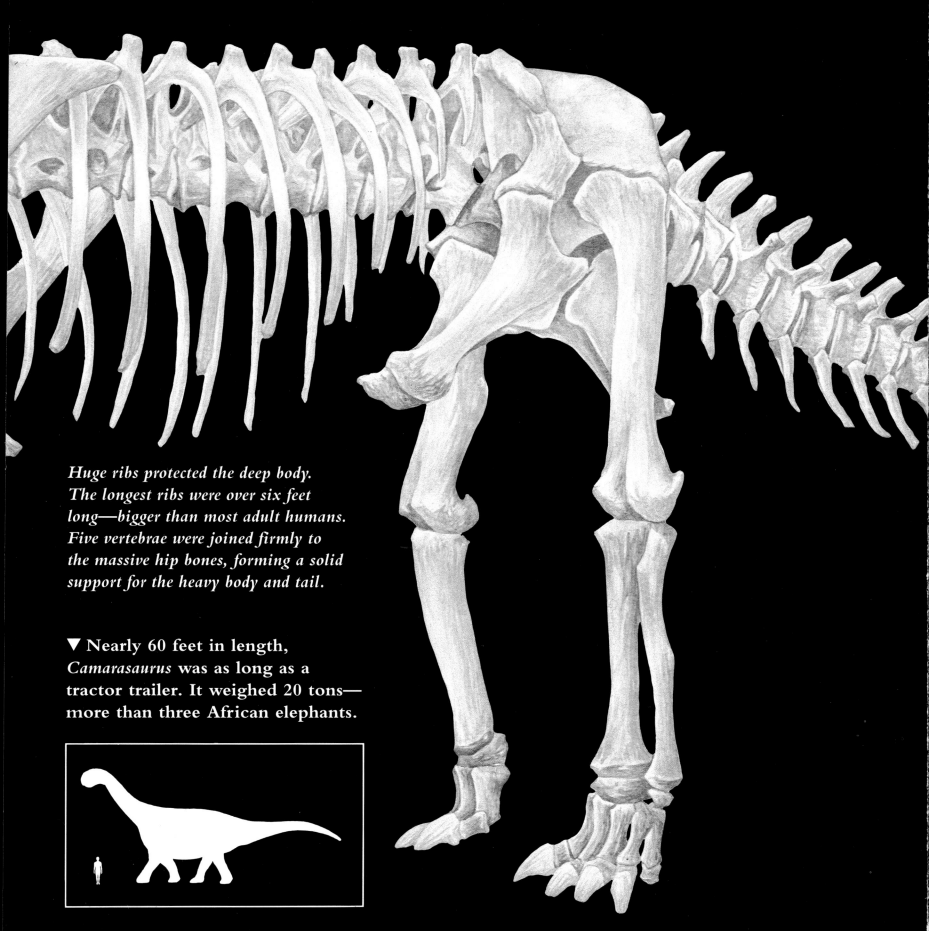

Huge ribs protected the deep body.
The longest ribs were over six feet
long—bigger than most adult humans.
Five vertebrae were joined firmly to
the massive hip bones, forming a solid
support for the heavy body and tail.

▼ **Nearly 60 feet in length,**
***Camarasaurus* was as long as a**
tractor trailer. It weighed 20 tons—
more than three African elephants.

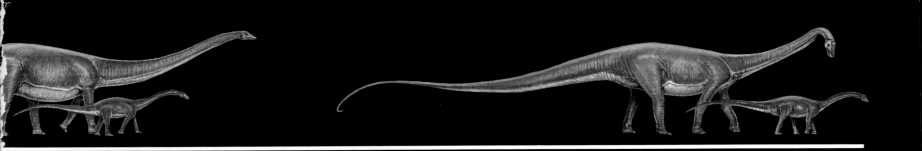

The special structure of its vertebrae make **Diplodocus** light for its size. The vertebrae are partly hollow, so they weigh less than if they were made of solid bone.

The hip bones of Diplodocus had to be extremely strong to bear the weight of the body and tail. The five vertebrae above the hip bone were joined together to add more support.

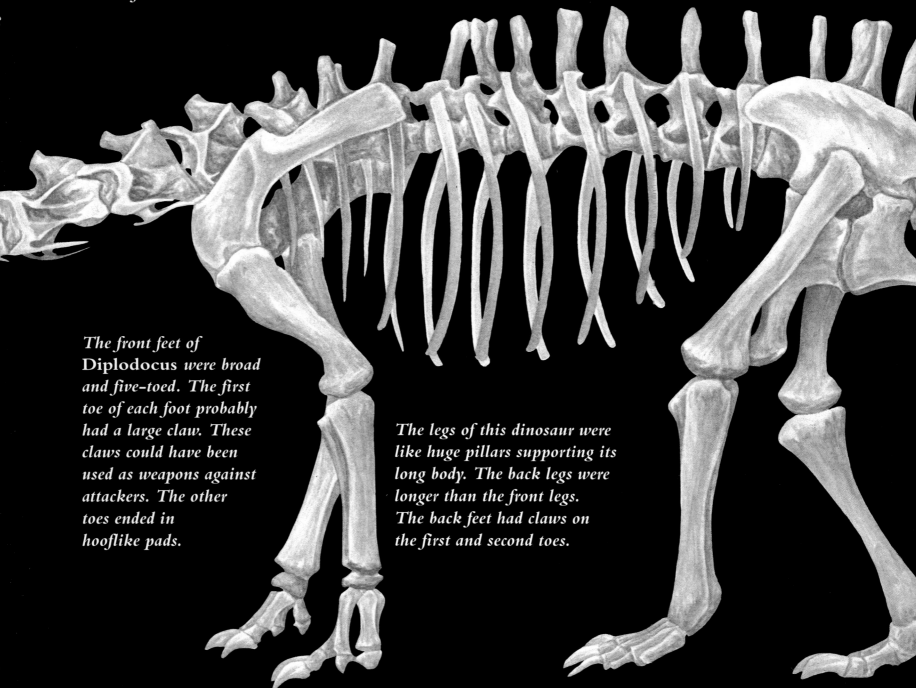

The front feet of **Diplodocus** were broad and five-toed. The first toe of each foot probably had a large claw. These claws could have been used as weapons against attackers. The other toes ended in hooflike pads.

The legs of this dinosaur were like huge pillars supporting its long body. The back legs were longer than the front legs. The back feet had claws on the first and second toes.

DIPLODOCUS

One of the largest land animals that ever lived was *Diplodocus*. It belonged to the diplodocid family of long-necked dinosaurs, or sauropods, which also included the weighty *Apatosaurus*.

The sheer bulk of this peaceful plant eater protected it from most enemies. Only predators such as *Allosaurus*, the biggest meat-eating dinosaur of the time, would have been able to attack such a giant.

Diplodocus walked on four legs. It was not a fast mover. Its build and the footprints that have been found suggest that it walked at about the same speed as a human. Tracks also suggest that *Diplodocus* lived in herds as elephants do today. Young animals would have been protected by the adults in the herd (see the illustrations at the top of the page).

Vertebrae

The broad head of Diplodocus *was small for such a giant animal. At just over two feet long, it was not much bigger than a horse's head. At the front of the mouth were rows of fine, closely packed teeth. The nostrils were right at the top of the head. In this position they were well out of the way of twigs and branches.*

The neck of Diplodocus *was about 24 feet long and contained 15 vertebrae.*

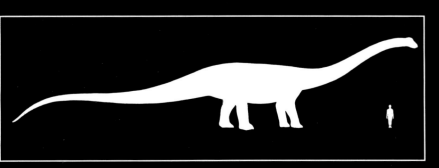

◀ Although *Diplodocus* was more than 88 feet long—longer than a line of seven cars—it weighed only 11 tons, or slightly more than two African elephants. *Apatosaurus*, a relative of *Diplodocus*, was shorter but weighed about 30 tons.

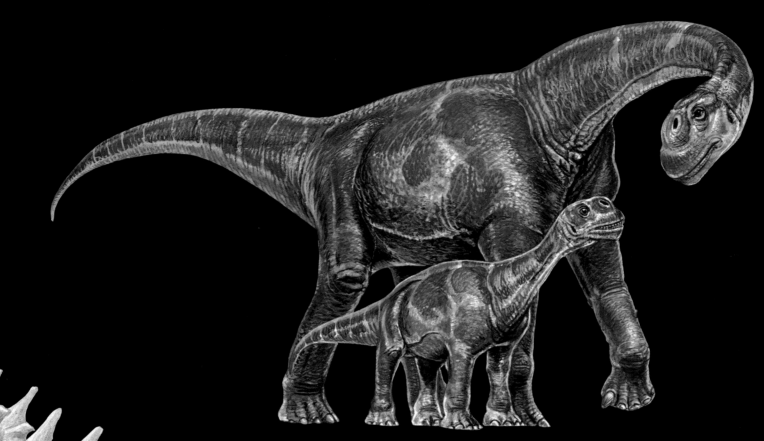

HERD DWELLER

Some 156 to 144 million years ago, in the late Jurassic period, groups of *Camarasaurus* roamed the moist tropical plains of western North America. These massive creatures moved in herds, which helped keep the young safe from attack by flesh-eating dinosaurs.

The tail of Camarasaurus was short in comparison to that of other sauropods. It contained about 54 vertebrae, while some other sauropods had as many as 80. The V-shaped bones below the tail vertebrae protected blood vessels on the underside of the tail.

IGUANODON

This dinosaur's long skull ended in a powerful, toothless beak for chopping off mouthfuls of plant food. Farther back in the broad snout were plenty of strong teeth—useful for chewing tough plants. New teeth developed as old ones wore out.

A large, slow-moving plant eater, *Iguanodon* was the second dinosaur to be discovered. Part of a leg bone was found in England in 1809, and many more bones and some teeth were found in 1822. When scientists first put *Iguanodon* together, they placed the dinosaur's thumb spike on its nose, believing it to be a horn.

Iguanodon was a member of a family of heavily built animals known as iguanodonts, which lived all over the world. These dinosaurs could walk on two legs but also moved on all four.

Fossil footprints show that *Iguanodon* traveled in herds for safety. Smaller predators would not have dared to attack a group of these mighty creatures. Also, a threatened *Iguanodon* could run at about 20 miles an hour on two legs or, if need be, defend itself with its thumb spike.

On each hand Iguanodon had a sharp spike instead of a thumb. The animal used it to jab at the eye or neck of an attacker. The three middle fingers were like pointed hooves; Iguanodon used these when it walked on all fours. The fifth finger could be bent across the palm and used to grasp food.

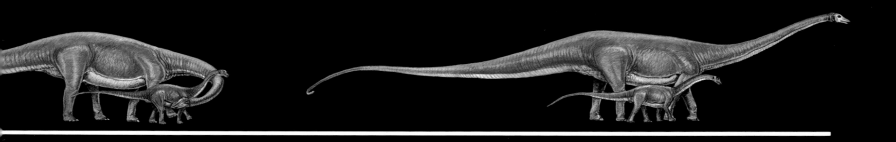

PLANT-EATING GIANT

Diplodocus lived in western North America about 140 million years ago, during the late Jurassic period. A plant eater, its fine teeth would have been ideal for stripping leaves from plants but not for chewing. The discovery of smooth pebbles near the fossils of these dinosaurs suggests that sauropods swallowed stones to help grind up food inside their stomachs. Birds today swallow grit and small stones for the same reason.

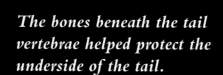

The bones beneath the tail vertebrae helped protect the underside of the tail.

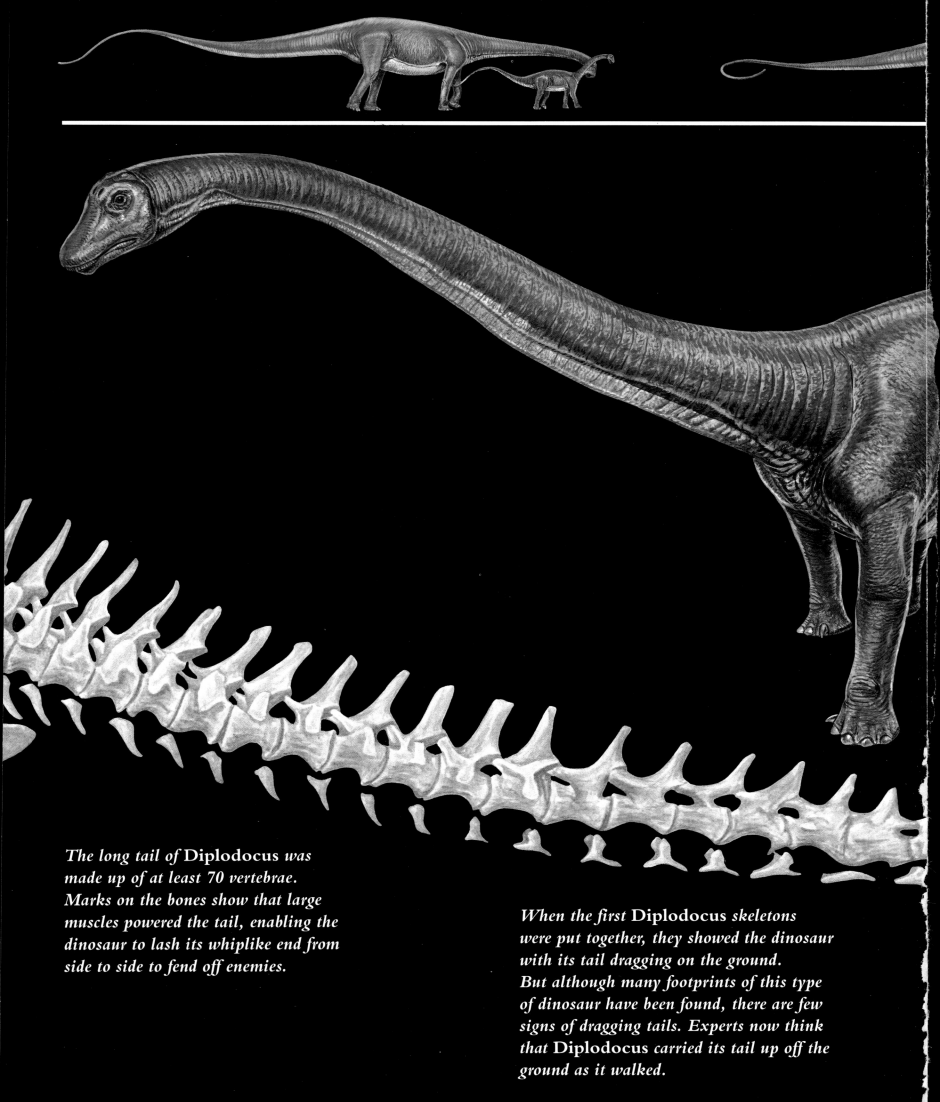

The long tail of **Diplodocus** *was made up of at least 70 vertebrae. Marks on the bones show that large muscles powered the tail, enabling the dinosaur to lash its whiplike end from side to side to fend off enemies.*

When the first **Diplodocus** *skeletons were put together, they showed the dinosaur with its tail dragging on the ground. But although many footprints of this type of dinosaur have been found, there are few signs of dragging tails. Experts now think that* **Diplodocus** *carried its tail up off the ground as it walked.*

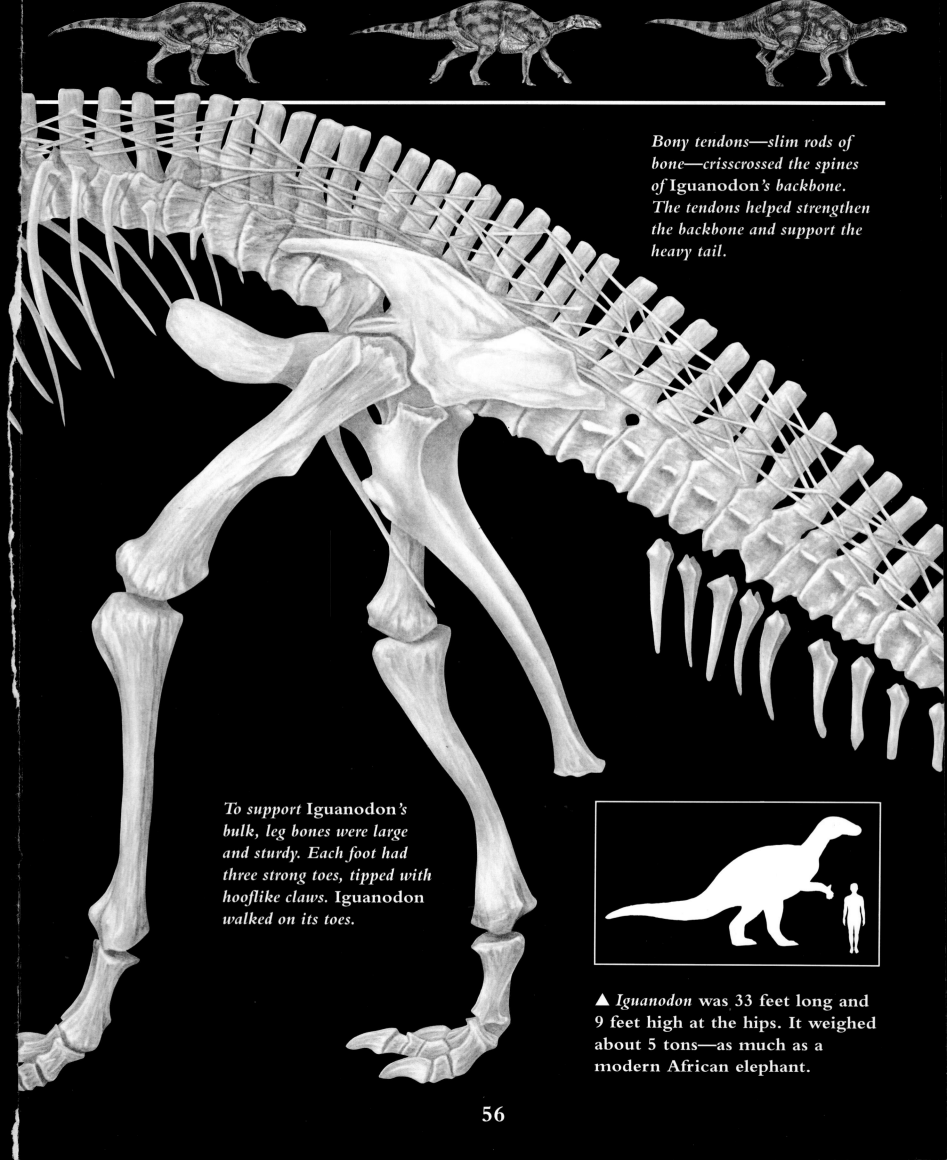

Bony tendons—slim rods of bone—crisscrossed the spines of Iguanodon's backbone. The tendons helped strengthen the backbone and support the heavy tail.

To support Iguanodon's bulk, leg bones were large and sturdy. Each foot had three strong toes, tipped with hooflike claws. Iguanodon walked on its toes.

▲ Iguanodon was 33 feet long and 9 feet high at the hips. It weighed about 5 tons—as much as a modern African elephant.

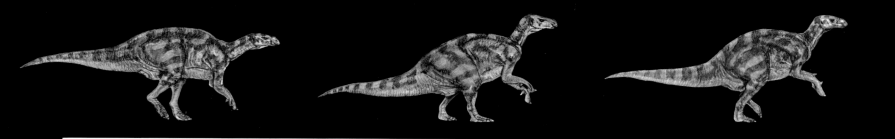

PEACEFUL PLANT EATER

Herds of *Iguanodon* roamed Europe during the early Cretaceous period, 128 to 108 million years ago. They browsed on such plants as ferns and horsetails growing along rivers and streams. An *Iguanodon* could also feed on tree foliage if it stood up on its two hind legs, using its long tail as a prop.

A heavy tail held straight out behind the body helped balance **Iguanodon**'s *weight when it walked on two legs.*

V-shaped bones below the tail protected the blood vessels that ran underneath the backbone.

TYRANNOSAURUS

Massive and ferocious, *Tyrannosaurus* is the biggest hunting animal known to have lived on land. It was the largest of the carnosaurs—the big, flesh-eating dinosaurs of the Jurassic and Cretaceous periods. All carnosaurs were bulky animals with powerful jaws and sharp teeth.

Tyrannosaurus walked upright on its two back legs and may have moved at 20 miles an hour or more. With its huge, heavy body, it could not chase prey for long. Instead, it stayed hidden among trees and waited for victims to come near. *Tyrannosaurus* then leapt out and charged toward its prey, killing it with fierce bites to the neck. Plant-eating dinosaurs such as *Edmontosaurus* and *Ankylosaurus* were probably its main food.

Tyrannosaurus also found food by scavenging—feeding on dead animals or taking prey from other predators.

The skeleton of an animal as large as Tyrannosaurus *had to be big enough to support its vast bulk but not so heavy that the animal could not move quickly enough to catch prey.*

▼ *Tyrannosaurus* was about 40 feet long and 12 feet tall. When rearing up on its hind legs, this fierce meat-eating dinosaur reached 18 feet. It weighed six or seven tons—more than an African elephant today.

Like other dinosaurs that walked on two legs, Tyrannosaurus *held its long tail straight out behind it. This helped balance the weight of the front part of its body, including its massive head.*

The back leg bones were big and strong to support the heavy body. The ankle bones were fairly long, enabling it to move quickly over a short distance.

Each of the dinosaur's broad back feet had four toes—one small and three large toes, all with heavy claws.

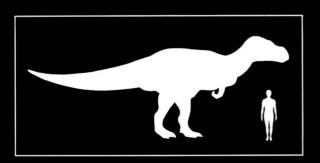

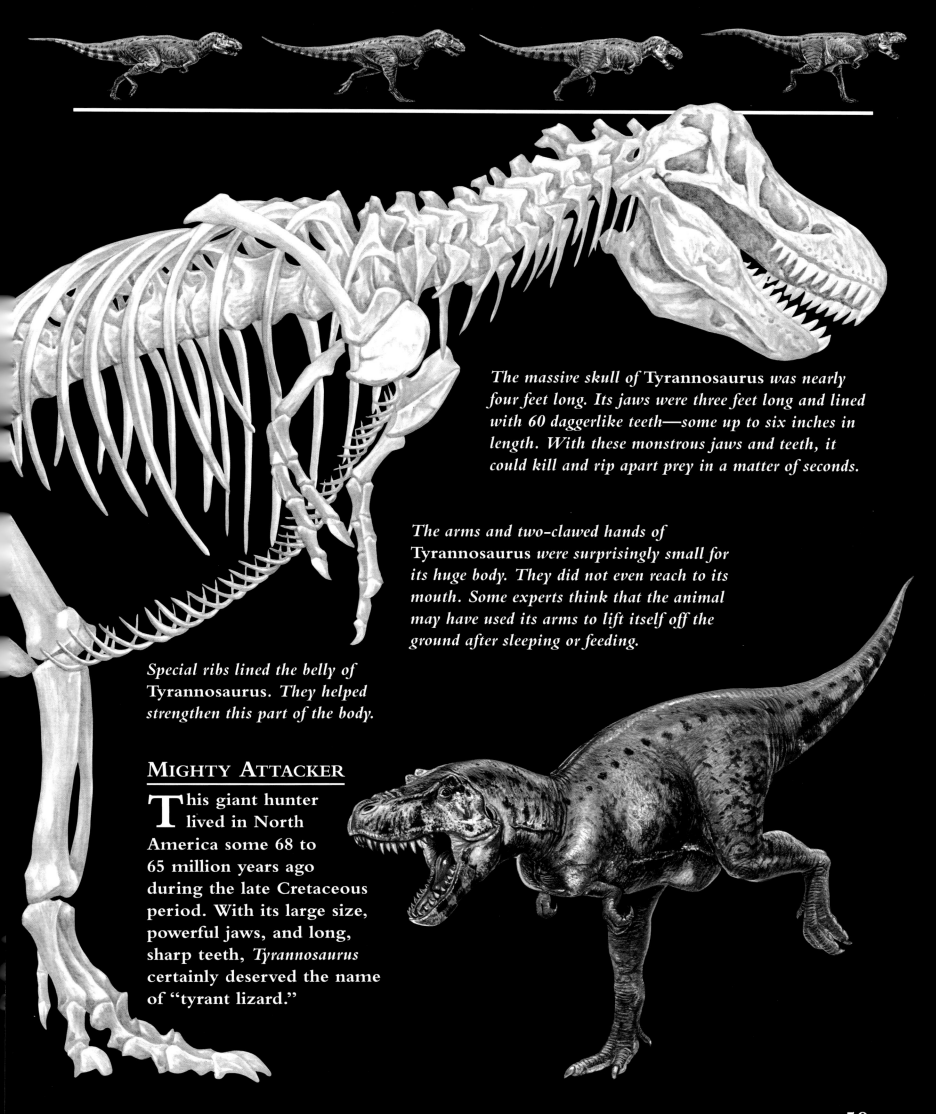

The massive skull of **Tyrannosaurus** *was nearly four feet long. Its jaws were three feet long and lined with 60 daggerlike teeth—some up to six inches in length. With these monstrous jaws and teeth, it could kill and rip apart prey in a matter of seconds.*

The arms and two-clawed hands of **Tyrannosaurus** *were surprisingly small for its huge body. They did not even reach to its mouth. Some experts think that the animal may have used its arms to lift itself off the ground after sleeping or feeding.*

Special ribs lined the belly of **Tyrannosaurus.** *They helped strengthen this part of the body.*

MIGHTY ATTACKER

This giant hunter lived in North America some 68 to 65 million years ago during the late Cretaceous period. With its large size, powerful jaws, and long, sharp teeth, *Tyrannosaurus* certainly deserved the name of "tyrant lizard."

LAMBEOSAURUS

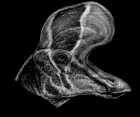

A large, sturdy plant eater, *Lambeosaurus* belonged to a group of dinosaurs called hadrosaurs. These dinosaurs are also known as duckbills because of their long, flattened, horn-covered beak.

Some hadrosaurs had flat heads. Others had oddly shaped crests on the tops of their heads. Different species had crests of different shapes, as you can see in the pictures at the top of the page. It is possible that the crests of males and females of the same species varied in shape and size.

Hollow passages inside the crest may have acted like echo chambers to make the hadrosaur's booming calls even louder. The shape of the crest affected the sound, so each kind of hadrosaur may have had its own call. Hadrosaurs lived in herds, and experts think that their crests and calls helped them to recognize and keep in touch with others of their own species as well as to find mates.

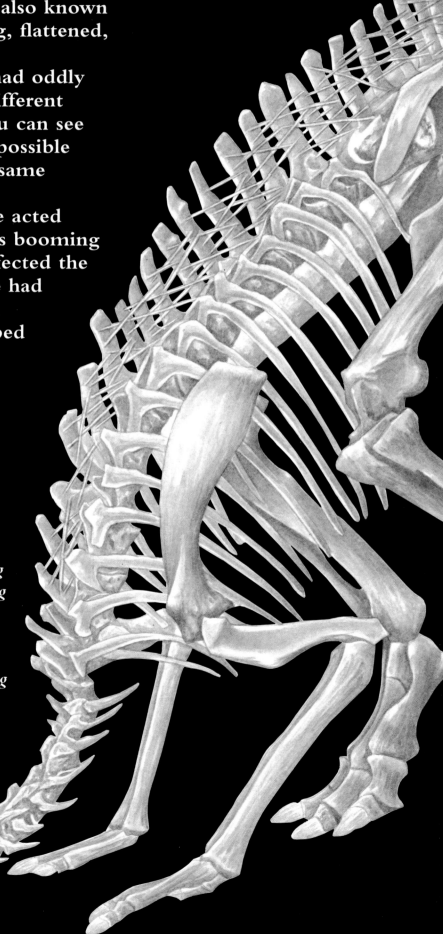

Lambeosaurus had two structures on its head—a tall, hollow crest and a solid, bony spike behind it.

The neck was strong yet flexible, allowing Lambeosaurus *to gather low-growing plants from a wide area without having to move too much.*

Like all hadrosaurs, Lambeosaurus *used its toothless beak to nip off plant food. It then chewed the food with the teeth farther back in its jaws.*

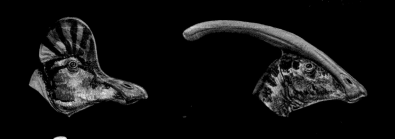

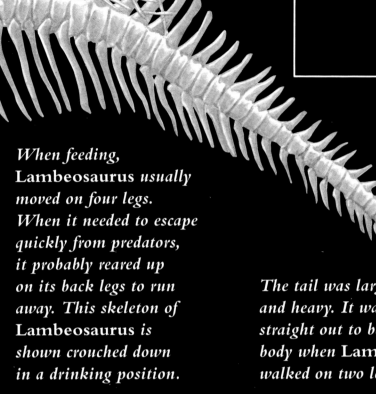

Lambeosaurus measured about 33 feet from nose to tail—as long as three cars. It weighed as much as three tons.

When feeding, Lambeosaurus usually moved on four legs. When it needed to escape quickly from predators, it probably reared up on its back legs to run away. This skeleton of Lambeosaurus is shown crouched down in a drinking position.

The tail was large and heavy. It was held straight out to balance the body when Lambeosaurus walked on two legs.

GROUP NESTER

Lambeosaurus lived in North America some 76 million years ago during the late Cretaceous period. The remains of nests found together suggest that some types of hadrosaurs nested in groups. Each female scraped a hollow in the earth to make a safe pit for her eggs. Once hatched, the young dinosaurs probably stayed in the nesting colony while the parents found food to bring them.

STEGOCERAS

The top of the eight-inch-long skull was a high dome of solid bone. This took the force of the impact when **Stegoceras** crashed head on into a rival. The domes grew larger with age, and males had bigger domes than females.

The back vertebrae had special joints that held them tightly locked together and prevented them from twisting out of line during head-crashing battles. Thin, bony rods, or tendons, running between the vertebrae strengthened the back further.

The jaws of **Stegoceras** contained slightly curved, jagged-edged teeth. These were ideally shaped for tearing up plant food.

Special ribs lined the belly and helped strengthen this part of the body.

Although peaceful creatures for most of the time, male *Stegoceras* dinosaurs probably took part in fierce battles during the mating season. They charged toward one another with head lowered and neck, body, and tail held straight out (see pictures at the top of the page). The rivals clashed head on, and the thickened bony dome on their heads acted as a built-in crash helmet to protect them. Some experts think the beasts also rammed each other's sides.

Stegoceras belonged to a family of dinosaurs called pachycephalosaurs, which means "thick-headed lizards." The largest pachycephalosaurs had skulls capped with solid bone up to ten inches thick. Many also had bony frills and spikes around the dome.

Stegoceras *moved upright on its two back legs. Its arms were much shorter and were used to handle food.*

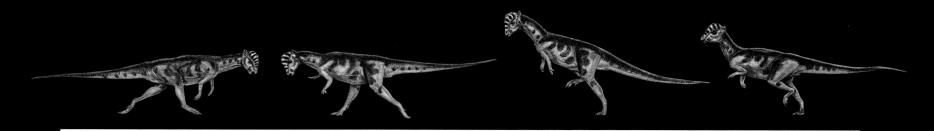

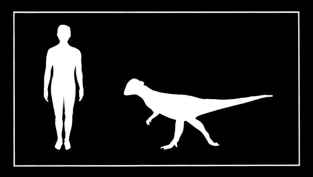

When held straight out, the heavy tail of this dinosaur helped balance the weight of its domed head.

▲ From its head to the end of its tail, *Stegoceras* measured about six feet long.

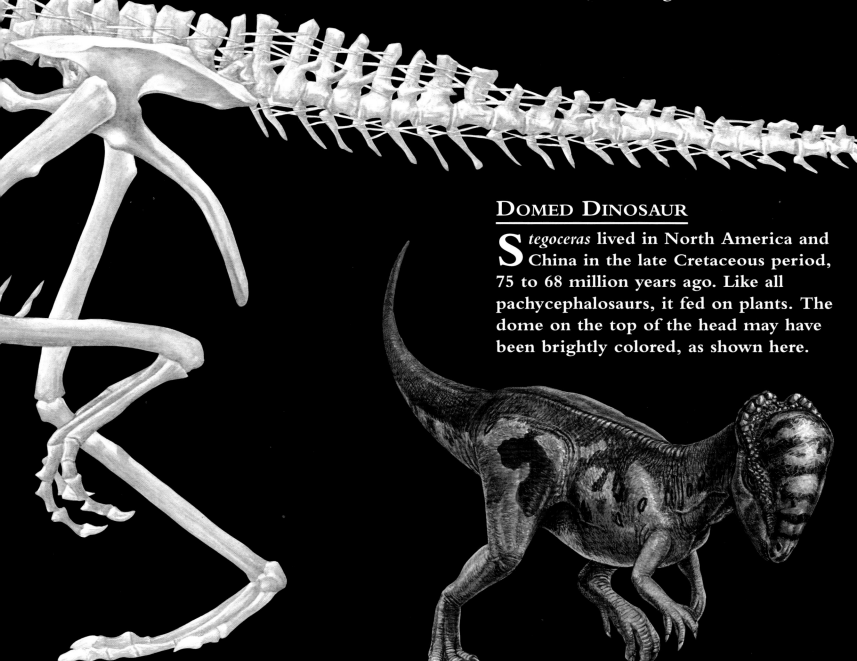

DOMED DINOSAUR

S tegoceras lived in North America and China in the late Cretaceous period, 75 to 68 million years ago. Like all pachycephalosaurs, it fed on plants. The dome on the top of the head may have been brightly colored, as shown here.

STEGOSAURUS

One of the most easily recognized of all dinosaurs, *Stegosaurus* was the biggest of the group known as stegosaurs, or "plated dinosaurs." Typical of its kind, *Stegosaurus* was a large, slow-moving plant eater with a small head. Its huge body was topped with double rows of large, bony plates.

What was the purpose of these flattened bones? Many experts now think that they were a way of controlling body temperature. Blood-rich skin may have covered the plates. When a *Stegosaurus* was cold, it would turn its side toward the sun. The sun's heat would warm the blood as it passed over the plates on its way around the body. When facing away from the sun and into a breeze, the plates would give off heat and thus cool the animal.

The plates on the back of Stegosaurus were probably arranged in two alternating rows, as shown here. People used to think they were arranged in pairs. The largest plates were two feet wide and two feet tall.

Stegosaurus *had an extremely small skull for such a large animal. The skull was only about 16 inches long and protected a brain the size of a walnut.*

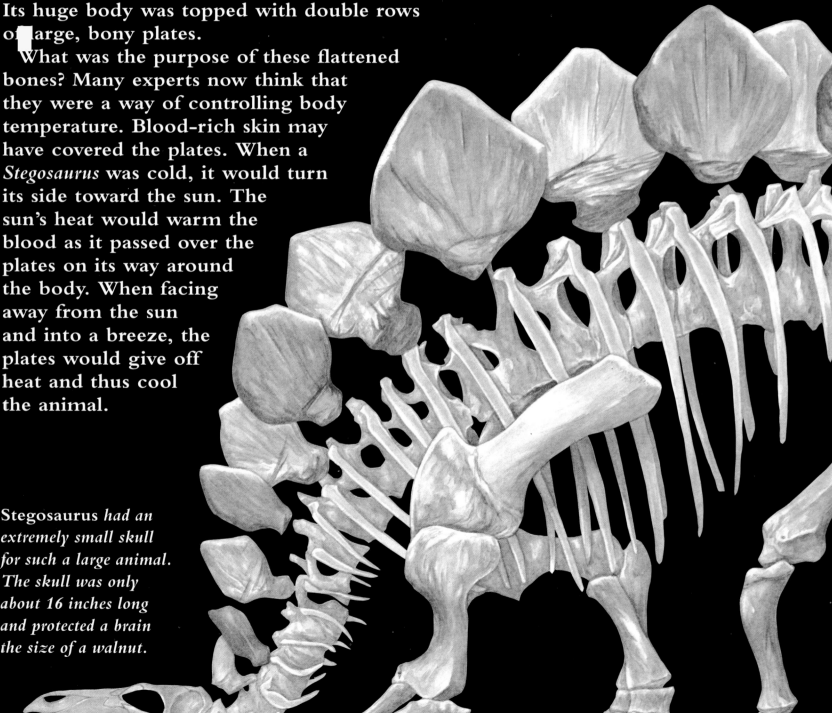

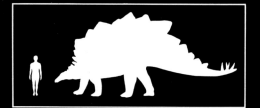

◄ At more than 24 feet long, *Stegosaurus* was longer than an African elephant and weighed as much as two tons.

PLANT EATER

Although *Stegosaurus* usually moved on four legs, it may have reared up on two legs to feed on the branches of trees, as shown here. *Stegosaurus* lived in western North America 156 to 144 million years ago during the late Jurassic period. Other kinds of stegosaurs lived in Europe, Africa, and China.

The massive back legs were more than twice as long as the front legs, so the body of Stegosaurus sloped forward from its highest point at the hips. The broad, three-toed feet helped spread the body's great weight. Short front legs allowed the head on its short neck to be brought down to the ground for feeding. The front feet had five strong, clawed toes.

At the end of the tail were foot-long spikes covered in tough horn, like the horns of cattle. Stegosaurus defended itself by lashing attackers with this spiked tail.

65

EUOPLOCEPHALUS

Studded with spikes and horns and armed with a tail ending in a bony club, *Euoplocephalus* was built like a tank and able to defend itself against most enemies. Its heavy body was covered with plates of bone set into its leathery skin, making it difficult to bite or attack. Even its eyelids were armored—pieces of bone came down like shutters over the normal lids to protect the eyes from sharp claws. A predator's only chance was to try and turn *Euoplocephalus* over onto its back—its undersides were less well protected than the rest of its body.

Euoplocephalus belonged to the ankylosaur, or "armored dinosaur," group. They were sturdy creatures with clublike tails. *Euoplocephalus* moved on four legs and fed on plants, nipping leaves off with the toothless beak at the front of its broad head.

The body, sides, and front legs of Euoplocephalus *were protected by rows of triangular spikes jutting out of the skin.*

Horn

Euoplocephalus *had an extremely strong skull, with a covering of extra pieces of bone. At the back of the skull were short, triangular horns giving more protection to the head.*

CLUB-TAILED DINOSAUR

Euoplocephalus lived in North America 80 to 70 million years ago during the late Cretaceous period. If attacked while it searched for food, this ankylosaur would lash out with its clublike tail. A blow from this bony weapon could injure even a large predator, such as *Tyrannosaurus*.

The club on the end of the tail was made up of two large balls of bone joined together. The bones of the tail were stiffened and strengthened with bony tendons—thin bony rods— to support the heavy club.

Heavy hipbones carried large powerful muscles. These helped Euoplocephalus *swing its clubbed tail from side to side. The club weighed more than 60 pounds—as much as a seven-year-old child.*

▼ Including its long tail, *Euoplocephalus* measured about 20 feet in length. It weighed about two tons.

Sturdy leg bones helped support the weight of this heavily armored dinosaur. Euoplocephalus *was agile for its size and able to run away from danger.*

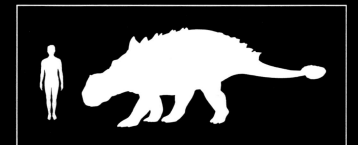

TRICERATOPS

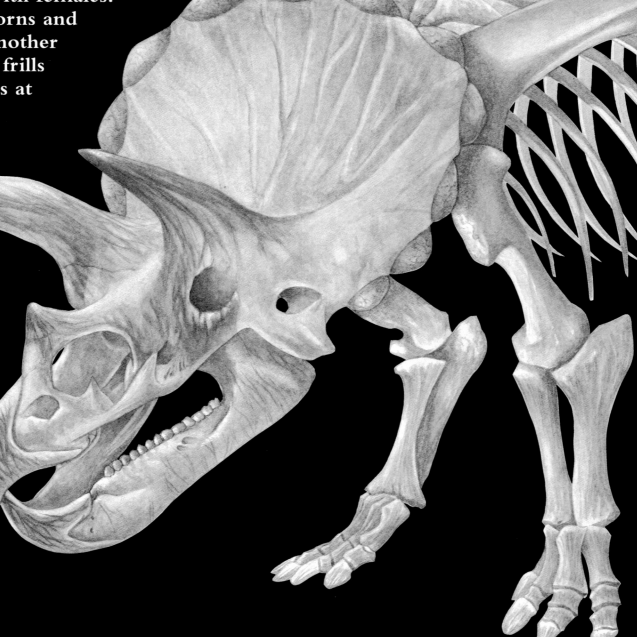

Long, sharp horns and a bony frill around its neck kept *Triceratops* safe from the fiercest of enemies—even *Tyrannosaurus*. If threatened, this horned creature charged like a giant rhinoceros.

Triceratops was one of the largest of the group known as ceratopsians, or "horned dinosaurs." A large, heavy plant eater, it roamed the forests to find food. It was not a fast mover and did not rely on speed for defense.

Male *Triceratops* also used their sharp horns to battle for leadership of the herd and the chance to mate with females. Rival males locked horns and pushed against one another with their bony neck frills (shown in the pictures at the top of the page).

The neck frill was a solid sheet of bone. It acted as a protective shield for the neck and shoulders. The frill may have been brightly colored.

The huge skull of Triceratops *measured up to seven feet from the nose to the back of the head. The two horns on the brow were around three feet long, and the short horn on the nose measured about seven inches.*

At the front of the mouth was a sharp beak. Triceratops *used this to bite off mouthfuls of tough plants. The food was then chewed farther back in the jaws with its grinding teeth.*

◀ *Triceratops* **was 30 feet long, 10 feet tall, and 9 tons in weight. Imagine an animal twice the length of a rhinoceros and heavier than a full-grown African elephant.**

Hips

HORNED GIANT

Massive *Triceratops* wandered western North America 68 to 65 million years ago, during the late Cretaceous period. If threatened, it would use its massive horned head to ward off its attacker.

The long hipbones of Triceratops *were attached to a greater than normal number of vertebrae— the bones that make up the backbone. This made the body stronger.*

Triceratops *walked on four legs. The leg bones of this dinosaur were thick and strong to carry the weight of its huge body and head.*

On the feet were short, wide toes— five on the front feet and four on the back—fanned out to help spread the animal's weight. They were the feet of a plodder, not a fast runner.

ICHTHYOSAURS

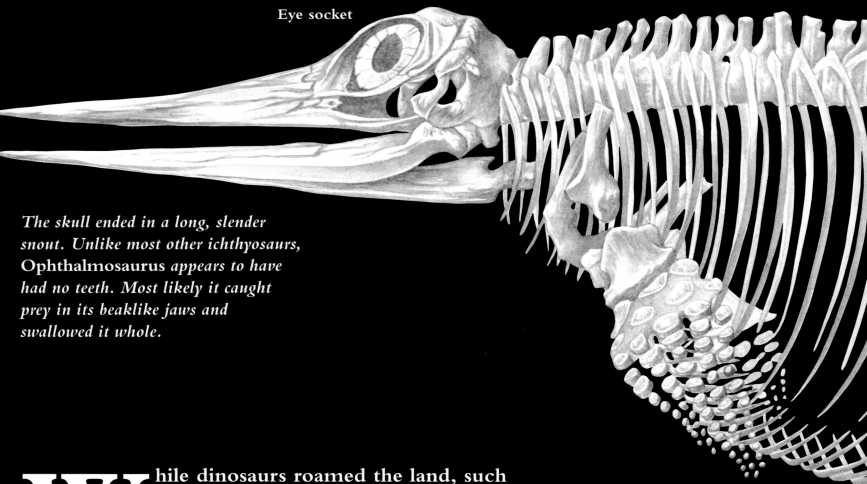

The skull ended in a long, slender snout. Unlike most other ichthyosaurs, Ophthalmosaurus *appears to have had no teeth. Most likely it caught prey in its beaklike jaws and swallowed it whole.*

The limbs of ichthyosaurs were shaped like paddles and were used for steering as they swam. The large front paddles were supported by extra bones.

While dinosaurs roamed the land, such sea-living reptiles as ichthyosaurs ruled the open waters. The name *ichthyosaur* means "fish lizard"; these reptiles look like fish because of their streamlined bodies and fishlike tails. The biggest ichthyosaur ever found was 50 feet long, but most measured only 6 to 12 feet long.

For about 100 million years, ichthyosaurs, such as *Ophthalmosaurus,* cruised the seas of the world. They lived much like today's dolphins, which are air-breathing mammals. Fast and agile, they could speed through the sea at up to 25 miles an hour. They hunted such prey as fish, squid, and the now-extinct squidlike belemnites. They also gave birth to their young in water.

Although they lived in the sea, ichthyosaurs were reptiles and had to come to the surface to breathe air. Their nostrils were set high up on the skull. This meant that the animals did not have to poke their heads far out of the water to breathe.

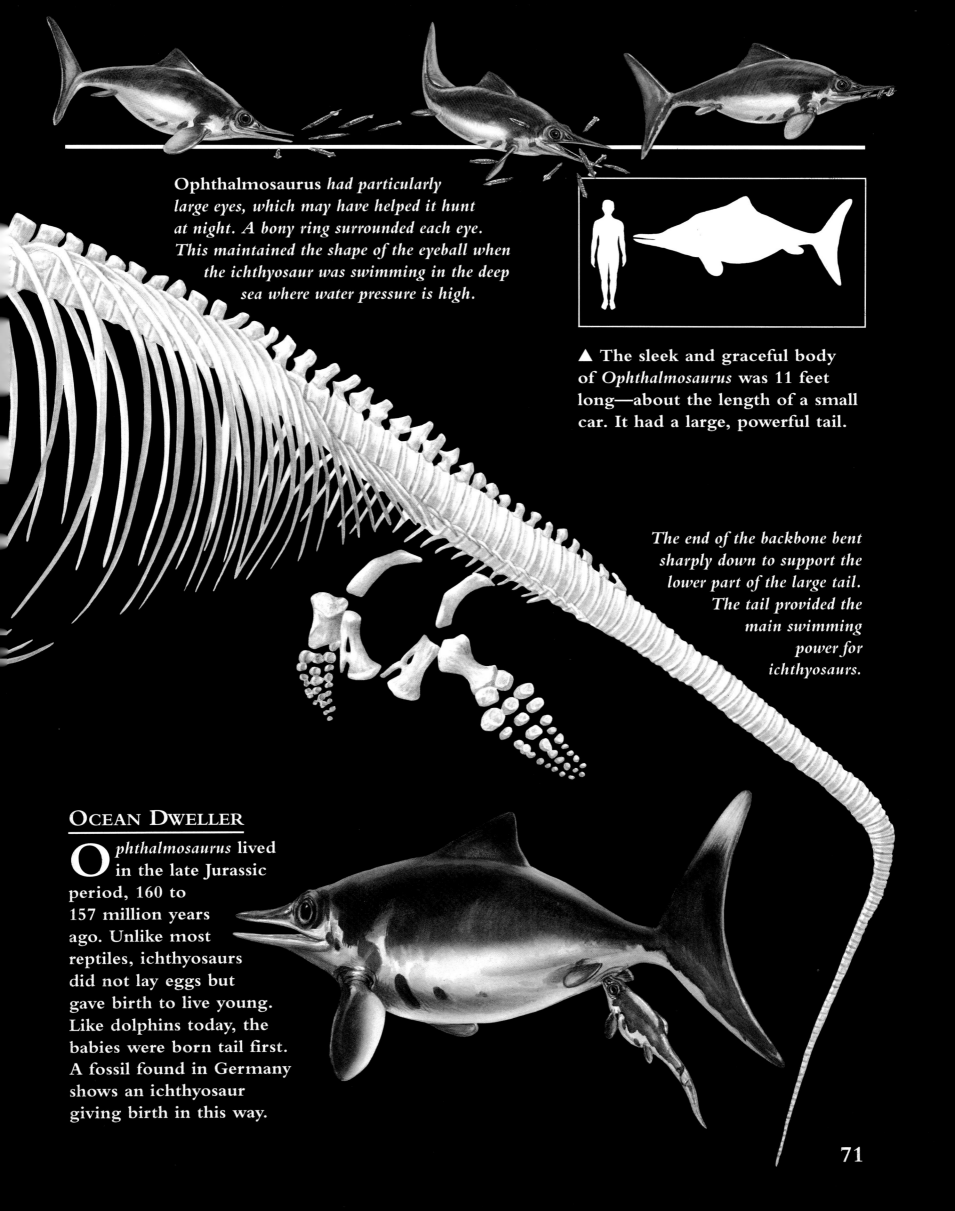

Ophthalmosaurus had particularly large eyes, which may have helped it hunt at night. A bony ring surrounded each eye. This maintained the shape of the eyeball when the ichthyosaur was swimming in the deep sea where water pressure is high.

▲ The sleek and graceful body of *Ophthalmosaurus* was 11 feet long—about the length of a small car. It had a large, powerful tail.

The end of the backbone bent sharply down to support the lower part of the large tail. The tail provided the main swimming power for ichthyosaurs.

OCEAN DWELLER

Ophthalmosaurus lived in the late Jurassic period, 160 to 157 million years ago. Unlike most reptiles, ichthyosaurs did not lay eggs but gave birth to live young. Like dolphins today, the babies were born tail first. A fossil found in Germany shows an ichthyosaur giving birth in this way.

PLESIOSAURS

Plesiosaurs were reptiles that lived in the sea at the same time that dinosaurs walked the earth. They were well adapted to aquatic life. Many kinds of plesiosaurs, such as *Cryptoclidus,* had small heads, long necks, and four paddle-shaped flippers. Like sea turtles today, they beat these flippers up and down in slow, steady movements to push themselves along in the water (see the pictures in the top panel).

Plesiosaurs spent nearly all their lives at sea, but they came to land to lay eggs. Like turtles, they dragged themselves up onto a beach and laid their eggs in pits that they made in the sand. When the young hatched, they made their own way down to the sea.

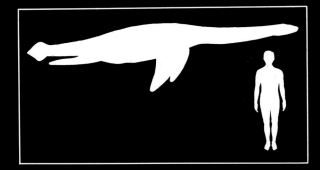

▲ Nose to tail, *Cryptoclidus* measured as much as 13 feet— longer than an average car. Some plesiosaurs were much larger—up to 46 feet long.

Belly ribs joined the shoulder bones and hip bones and made the plesiosaur's short body stronger and more rigid. This helped make a solid structure to support the powerful movements of the flippers.

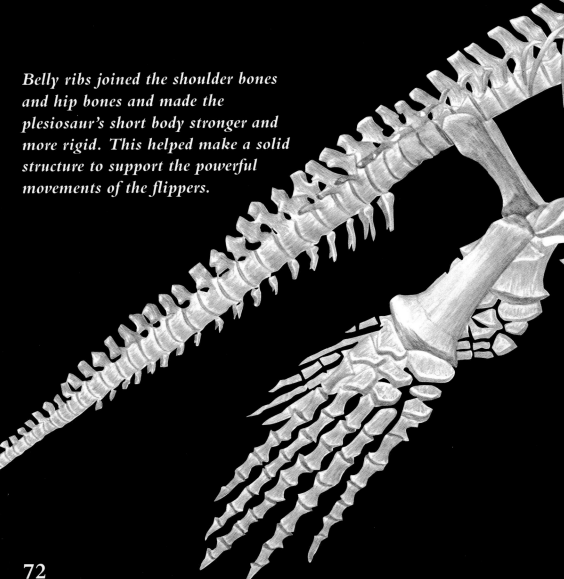

Belly ribs

Cryptoclidus *had long, narrow flippers instead of legs. In each toe, there were as many as ten bones. They helped make the flippers flexible.*

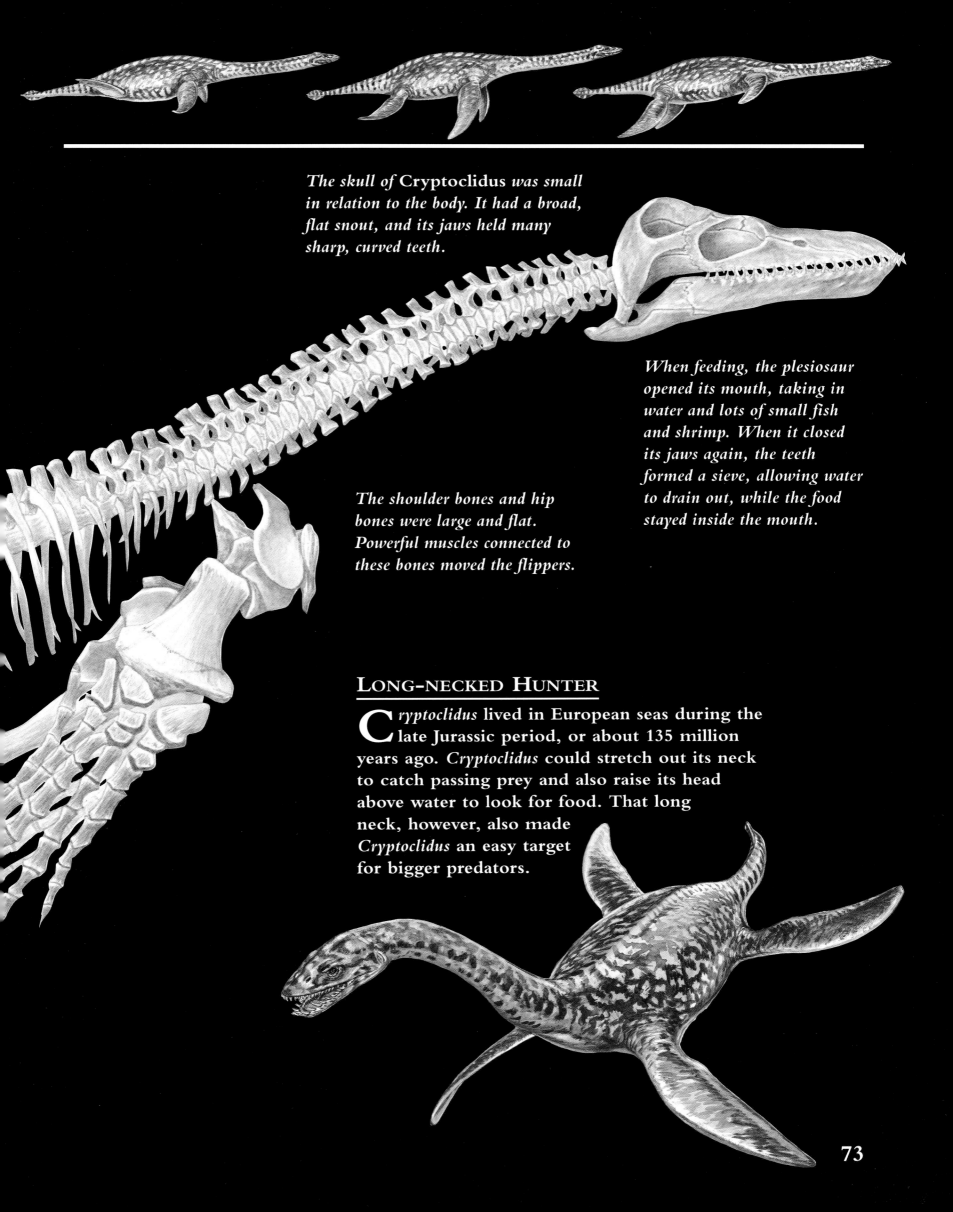

The skull of Cryptoclidus was small in relation to the body. It had a broad, flat snout, and its jaws held many sharp, curved teeth.

When feeding, the plesiosaur opened its mouth, taking in water and lots of small fish and shrimp. When it closed its jaws again, the teeth formed a sieve, allowing water to drain out, while the food stayed inside the mouth.

The shoulder bones and hip bones were large and flat. Powerful muscles connected to these bones moved the flippers.

LONG-NECKED HUNTER

Cryptoclidus lived in European seas during the late Jurassic period, or about 135 million years ago. *Cryptoclidus* could stretch out its neck to catch passing prey and also raise its head above water to look for food. That long neck, however, also made *Cryptoclidus* an easy target for bigger predators.

PTEROSAURS

When dinosaurs lived on land, flying reptiles called pterosaurs ruled the skies. As far as scientists know, pterosaurs were the first vertebrates—animals with backbones—to fly. They had wings made of skin attached to an extra long finger on each hand.

Pterosaurs ranged in size from small species about the size of a blackbird to the largest flying creatures ever. The biggest pterosaur was probably *Quetzalcoatlus*, which measured 40 feet from wing tip to wing tip—about the same wingspan as a light airplane's.

There were two kinds of pterosaurs. The earliest forms, called rhamphorhynchoids, had short legs and long, bony tails. Later came the pterodactyls, such as *Anhanguera*, which had short tails and longer necks and legs. Pterosaurs became extinct at the same time as the dinosaurs— about 64 million years ago.

Anhanguera's skull was nearly twice as long as its tiny body. On the top jaw was a crest that helped steady the head when the pterosaur plunged its jaws into water to catch fish.

The first three fingers of **Anhanguera's** *hand were short and tipped with sharp claws. The fourth finger was extremely long and supported the top edge of the wing. The wing was also attached to the side of the body, possibly at about hip level.*

Like all pterosaurs, Anhanguera *had an extremely light skeleton. Its bones were slender and many were hollow which made them even lighter.*

▼ The pterosaur *Anhanguera* measured 13 feet from wing tip to wing tip. It was bigger than a wandering albatross, the bird with the longest wings today, which has a wingspan of up to 11 feet. Although its wings were large, the body of this pterosaur was only 9–10 inches long.

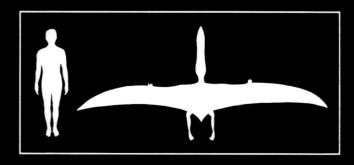

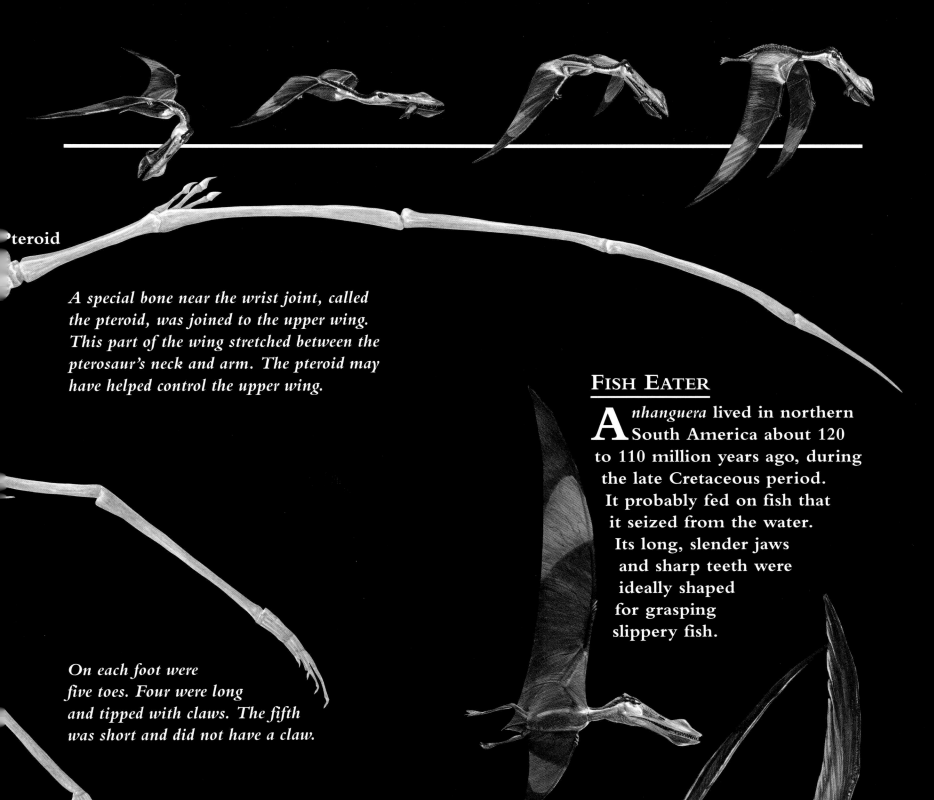

pteroid

A special bone near the wrist joint, called the pteroid, was joined to the upper wing. This part of the wing stretched between the pterosaur's neck and arm. The pteroid may have helped control the upper wing.

On each foot were five toes. Four were long and tipped with claws. The fifth was short and did not have a claw.

Experts disagree about how **Anhanguera** moved on the ground. Some believe that it walked upright on its two back feet like a modern bird. Others say that the structure of its hip bones shows that it could not have stood upright. They think that it crawled along using the claws on its front wings as well as its feet.

FISH EATER

Anhanguera lived in northern South America about 120 to 110 million years ago, during the late Cretaceous period. It probably fed on fish that it seized from the water. Its long, slender jaws and sharp teeth were ideally shaped for grasping slippery fish.

75

ARCHAEOPTERYX

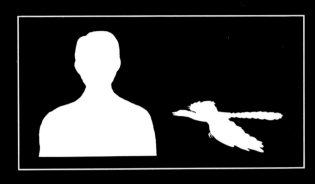

The earliest known bird, *Archaeopteryx,* was an extraordinary link between birds and reptiles such as dinosaurs. It had features of both groups. Like reptiles, *Archaeopteryx* had toothed jaws, a long, bony tail, and clawed fingers. Like birds, it had feathers on its wings and tail.

The first *Archaeopteryx* skeletons were found in 1861 in southern Germany. The detail of the fossil skeletons was so fine that an impression of feathers could be seen, proving that these creatures were not just small dinosaurs. The fossils showed that *Archaeopteryx* had wings just like those of birds today, and suggested that it would have been able to fly. But *Archaeopteryx* did not have the large breastbone of modern birds, which supports powerful flapping muscles. As a result, it probably could not flap up into the air from the ground but, instead, had to launch itself into the air from an elevated position such as the branch of a tree.

▲ *Archaeopteryx* was 14 inches long from head to tail—about the same size as a crow today.

TREE CLIMBER

Archaeopteryx lived in Europe about 150 million years ago, during the late Jurassic period. It fed on insects, flapping and gliding through the air in search of its prey. But *Archaeopteryx* could only fly for short periods and would have had to land on the ground. It would then have used its claws to climb up into trees in order to jump off into the air and fly again.

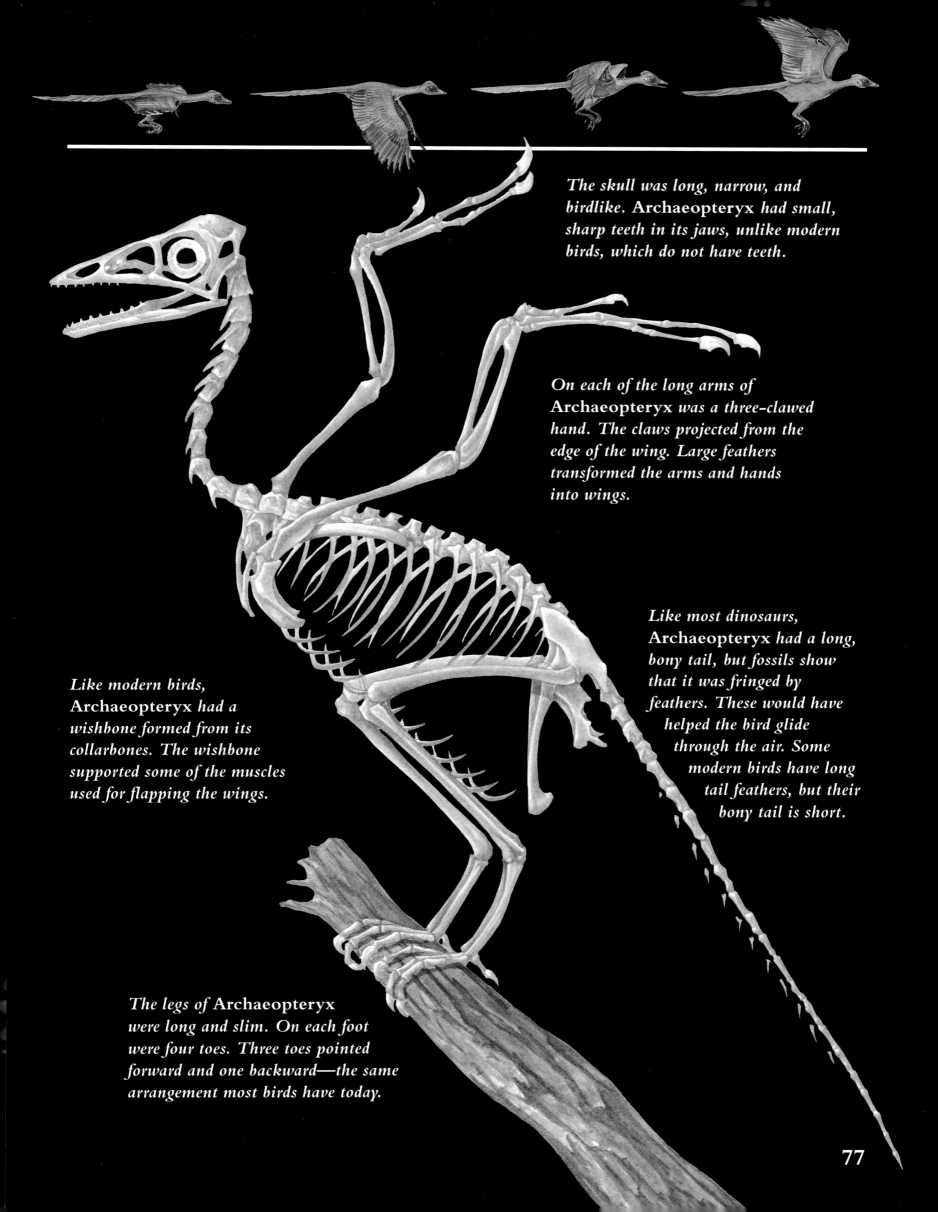

The skull was long, narrow, and birdlike. **Archaeopteryx** had small, sharp teeth in its jaws, unlike modern birds, which do not have teeth.

On each of the long arms of **Archaeopteryx** was a three-clawed hand. The claws projected from the edge of the wing. Large feathers transformed the arms and hands into wings.

Like most dinosaurs, **Archaeopteryx** had a long, bony tail, but fossils show that it was fringed by feathers. These would have helped the bird glide through the air. Some modern birds have long tail feathers, but their bony tail is short.

Like modern birds, **Archaeopteryx** had a wishbone formed from its collarbones. The wishbone supported some of the muscles used for flapping the wings.

The legs of Archaeopteryx were long and slim. On each foot were four toes. Three toes pointed forward and one backward—the same arrangement most birds have today.

77

GLOSSARY

AMPHIBIAN
A cold-blooded creature with a backbone and soft skin without scales that lives both in water and on land. Most amphibians lay eggs in water. The eggs hatch into swimming fishlike tadpoles. The tadpoles grow and change into adult animals, most of which can live on land. Amphibians include frogs, newts, and salamanders.

CARTILAGE
Tough, elastic material at the ends of bone and often part of the joints between bones. Smooth cartilage in joints helps them move more easily.

FIN
A flap on the body of a fish that pushes against the water when the fish moves. Dorsal fins are on the fish's back; ventral fins are on the belly. Pelvic fins and pectoral fins are both paired—there is one of each on each side of the body. Pectoral fins are just behind the head, and pelvic fins farther back.

FLIPPER
The paddlelike structure on the body of sea-living mammals, such as whales, seals, and plesiosaurs. Flippers are actually the animal's arms and legs changed into a shape more suitable for moving through water. (Some birds, such as penguins, use their wings as flippers.)

GILL
The opening on each side of a fish's head through which it breathes. As water flows into the mouth and out over the gills, the fish absorbs oxygen from the water.

GLAND
A part of the body that produces special substances, such as hormones or enzymes, which are passed into the blood, or poisons, which are passed to the outside of the body. A gland in a pit viper, for example, makes the poison that the snake injects into its victim as it bites.

HOOF
The thickened nail at the tip of a toe bone on which an animal walks. Horses have a single hoof on each foot—the tip of the third toe. Cattle have two hooves on each foot—the tips of the third and fourth toes.

KEEL
The large extension of the breastbone to which a bird's powerful flying muscles are attached.

MAMMAL
A warm-blooded animal with a backbone and a covering of fur or hair. Nearly all female mammals give birth to live young, which they feed with milk from their mammary glands. Mammals include dogs, cats, horses, and humans.

MARSUPIAL
A mammal that gives birth to its young before they are completely developed. Marsupial babies continue developing in a pouch on the mother's body. Marsupials include kangaroos, wallabies, and opossums.

MUSCLE
A bundle of fleshy fibers attached to bones in the body. The muscles contract—get shorter—to move parts of the body.

PRIMATE
Mammals with large brains and hands adapted for grasping. They include monkeys, chimpanzees, gorillas, and humans.

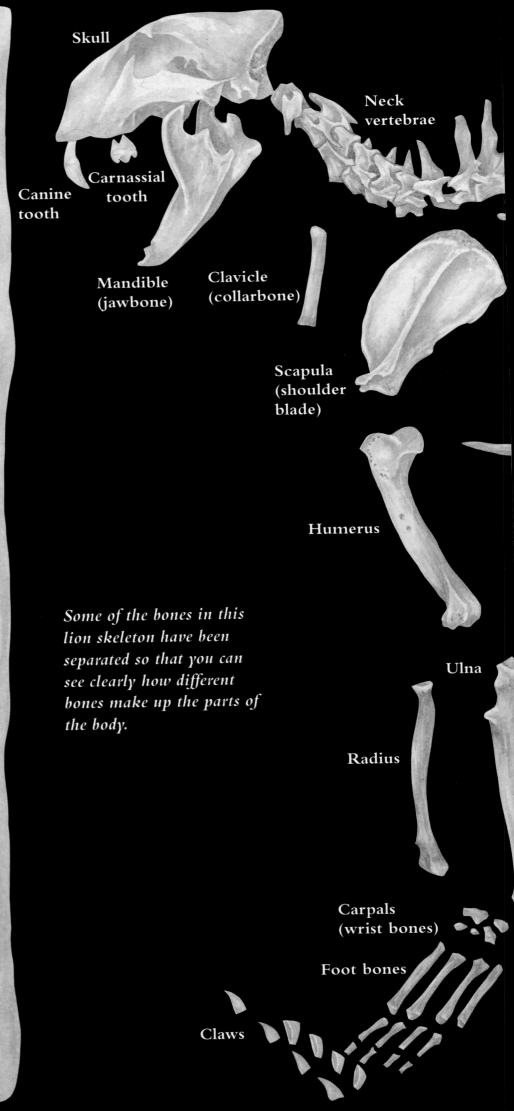

Skull

Neck vertebrae

Carnassial tooth

Canine tooth

Mandible (jawbone)

Clavicle (collarbone)

Scapula (shoulder blade)

Humerus

Ulna

Some of the bones in this lion skeleton have been separated so that you can see clearly how different bones make up the parts of the body.

Radius

Carpals (wrist bones)

Foot bones

Claws

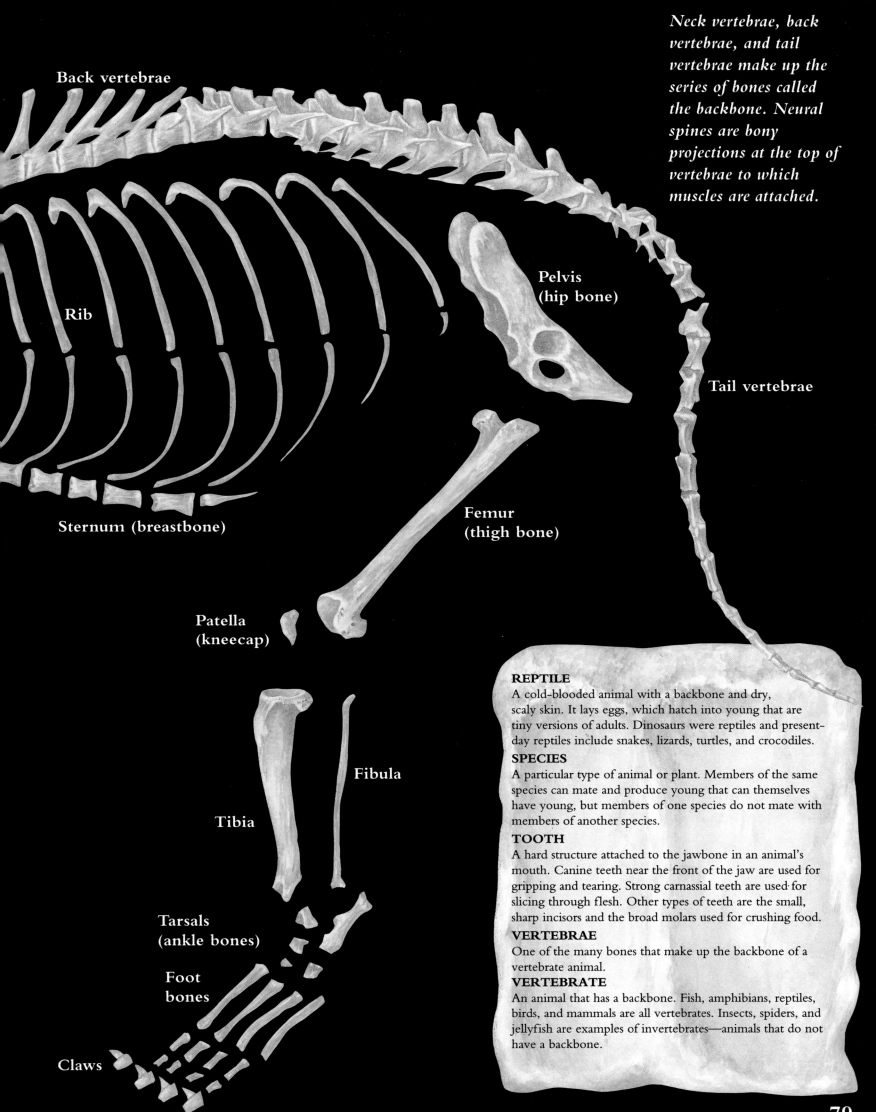

Back vertebrae

Rib

Sternum (breastbone)

Patella
(kneecap)

Tibia

Fibula

Tarsals
(ankle bones)

Foot
bones

Claws

Pelvis
(hip bone)

Tail vertebrae

Femur
(thigh bone)

Neck vertebrae, back vertebrae, and tail vertebrae make up the series of bones called the backbone. Neural spines are bony projections at the top of vertebrae to which muscles are attached.

REPTILE
A cold-blooded animal with a backbone and dry, scaly skin. It lays eggs, which hatch into young that are tiny versions of adults. Dinosaurs were reptiles and present–day reptiles include snakes, lizards, turtles, and crocodiles.

SPECIES
A particular type of animal or plant. Members of the same species can mate and produce young that can themselves have young, but members of one species do not mate with members of another species.

TOOTH
A hard structure attached to the jawbone in an animal's mouth. Canine teeth near the front of the jaw are used for gripping and tearing. Strong carnassial teeth are used for slicing through flesh. Other types of teeth are the small, sharp incisors and the broad molars used for crushing food.

VERTEBRAE
One of the many bones that make up the backbone of a vertebrate animal.

VERTEBRATE
An animal that has a backbone. Fish, amphibians, reptiles, birds, and mammals are all vertebrates. Insects, spiders, and jellyfish are examples of invertebrates—animals that do not have a backbone.

79

INDEX